Beautiful Ribbon Crafts

Home Decor · Wearables · Gift Wraps · Keepsakes · & More

Beautiful Ribbon Crafts

Home Decor · Wearables · Gift Wraps · Keepsakes · & More

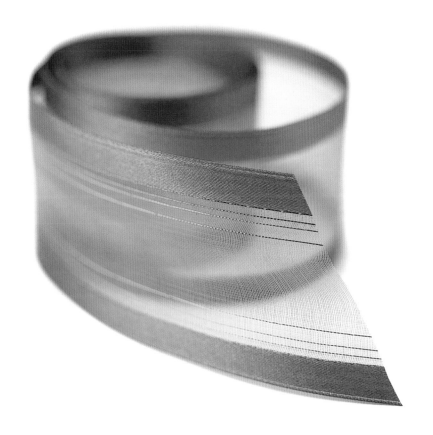

Marthe Le Van

LARK BOOKS

A Division of Sterling Publishing Company, Inc.

NEW YORK

Art Director:
Susan McBride

Assistant Art Director:
Hannes Charen

Cover Design:
Barbara Zaretsky

Assistant Editors:
Veronika Alice Gunter,
Rain Newcomb

Production Assistance:
Shannon Yokeley

Editorial Assistance:
Delores Gosnell

Photographer:
keithwright.com

Illustrator:
Orrin Lundgren

Special Photography:
Sanoma Syndication
Jeroen van der Spek, page 60;
Louis Lemaire, page 24;
Dolf Straatemeier, page 58;
George v.d. Wijngaard,
pages 76 and 96.

Library of Congress has cataloged the hardcover edition as follows:

Le Van, Marthe.
  Beautiful ribbon crafts : home decor, wearables, gift wraps, keepsakes & more/
Marthe Le Van.
    p. cm.
  ISBN 1-57990-358-4
  1. Ribbon work. I. Title.

TT850.5 .L47 2002
746'.0476--dc21
                           2002069508
10 9 8 7 6 5 4 3 2

Published by Lark Books, a division of
Sterling Publishing Co., Inc.
387 Park Avenue South, New York, N.Y. 10016

© 2003, Lark Books

Distributed in Canada by Sterling Publishing
c/o Canadian Manda Group, One Atlantic Ave., Suite 105
Toronto, Ontario, Canada M6K 3E7

Distributed in the U.K. by Guild of Master Craftsman Publications Ltd.
Castle Place, 166 High Street, Lewes, East Sussex, England BN7 1XU
Tel: (+ 44) 1273 477374, Fax: (+ 44) 1273 478606
Email: pubs@thegmcgroup.com, Web: www.gmcpublications.com

Distributed in Australia by Capricorn Link (Australia) Pty Ltd.
P.O. Box 704, Windsor, NSW 2756 Australia

If you have questions or comments about this book, please contact:
Lark Books
67 Broadway
Asheville, NC 28801
(828) 253-0467

Manufactured in China

ISBN 1-57990-358-4 (hardcover) 1-57990-556-0 (paperback)

Contents

Introduction...6

The Basics

Ribbon..8
Supplies & Tools...16
Techniques..18

The Projects

No-Sew Chic Napkin Rings...........................24
Zesty Mosaic Tray.......................................26
Sheer Bliss..28
Sun, Sand & Sea Tote..................................30
Versatile Orbs..32
Button & Bow Candle...................................34
Beaded Bookmark.......................................36
Beautiful Borders..38
Supernova Shade..40
Chopstick Pocket..42
24-Karat Bow...44
Azure Fields Bow..46
Woven Picture Frame...................................48
Buttercup & Gingham Linens.........................50
Rosy Ruffled Shade.....................................52
Folded Flower Pin.......................................54
Open-Weave Pillows & Blanket......................56
Table Rays...58
Celestial Cloth..60

Handcrafted Cards......................................62
Heart-to-Heart Sachet..................................66
Snapshot Scrapbook....................................68
Tapestry Pillow...70
Pleased-to-Meet-You Mat.............................72
Glamour Shade...74
Trace of Taffeta Wreath................................76
Summer Sun Hat...78
Perfect Vision Valet.....................................80
Keepsake Gift Bag.......................................82
Silky Lingerie Bag.......................................84
Picture Perfect Wall Hanging.........................87
Linen Place Mat & Napkin............................90
Pin Pillow..93
Periwinkle Passion Wreath............................96
Travel Pouch..98
Graceful Pleats Tieback..............................100
Bamboo Lamp..104
Imperial Pillow...107
Mediterranean Message Board.....................109
Scarf Seduction..112
Heavenly Table Topper...............................116
Drawstring Purse.......................................118
Nursery Cubbies.......................................120

Contributing Designers...............................124
Acknowledgments.....................................125
Index..127

Introduction

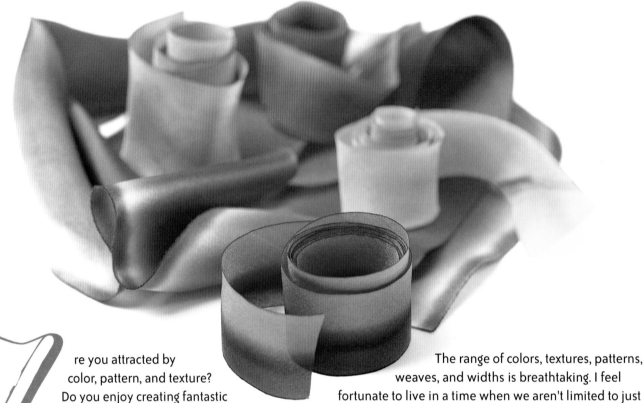

*A*re you attracted by color, pattern, and texture? Do you enjoy creating fantastic one-of-a-kind craft projects? Well then, get ready to fall head-over-heels in love with ribbon crafts. For anyone who thinks ribbon crafts are too traditional, require too many special skills, or are just plain frumpy, think again. The projects in this book, more than 40 in all, reflect a ribbon revolution. We're pleased to present a fresh variety of modern designs that crafters at any level can create. They're simple, fast, fun, and produce spectacular results. Included are contemporary home accents that everyone will adore, stylish wearables to complement your wardrobe, modern keepsakes your family will treasure, unique gift wrappings, and much, much more.

As a ribbon crafter, I often take as much time choosing the ribbons as making the project. Ribbons are eye candy to me, and shopping for ribbons is one of my favorite treats. As I walk down ribbon aisles, I'm amazed by the many varieties.

The range of colors, textures, patterns, weaves, and widths is breathtaking. I feel fortunate to live in a time when we aren't limited to just a few ribbon types, as crafters were not so long ago. Manufacturers have realized the popularity of ribbon crafting and met the challenge of producing a contemporary selection to delight and inspire.

No matter where you live, you can find a basic supply of ribbon. From gigantic discount retailers to craft stores to exclusive fabric shops to the Internet, ribbons are now big business. Although staple ribbons, such as satin and grosgrain, are very inexpensive, one can be easily seduced by much pricier ribbons, such as handwoven jacquards and hand-dyed silks. Fortunately you can achieve splendid effects by using just tiny lengths of these fine ribbons (see the Beautiful Borders on page 38 and the Perfect Vision Valet on page 80). As any ribbon lover can tell you, it's easy to become a collector, stashing away gorgeous or unusual bits and pieces of ribbon. (I'm always on the look out at antique stores

and rummage sales for vintage ribbons and other unique materials.) If you fit this description, please check out the Zesty Ribbon Tray on page 26 and the Handcrafted Cards on page 62. These "scrap" projects make excellent permanent ribbon displays.

With basic crafting skills, you can create each project in this book in just one day. However, it's wise to know a little bit about the different types of ribbon before you shop for materials, so we've included a glossary with photographs of the most common ribbon types and textures. You're likely to have most of the tools and supplies you'll need on hand—things like a pair of scissors, a pencil, a tape measure, and an iron are often called for. Since you may need to shop for fabric glue, fusible interfacing, and invisible thread, we've included descriptions of these materials. If you have a sewing machine and know how to use it, that's great. If not, feel free to hand-stitch any of the projects.

See how flexible ribbon crafts are? We also want you to feel like you have a lot of room to explore. That's why you should feel free to substitute any color or texture of ribbon that suits your fancy. No need to worry if you can't find the exact ribbon we used to make our projects, or if you wish to use an alternate ribbon. You can adapt all of our imaginative ideas to suit both ribbon availability and personal taste. We don't know your favorite color is blue, or that your niece's bedroom is purple, but you do, so go ahead and modify the projects to fit these preferences. We guarantee you'll have a lot more fun, and that's the true essence of ribbon crafts.

Enjoy!

The Basics

This chapter introduces you to the specific types of ribbons and what ribbons are best suited for what projects. You'll also find tips on cutting, handling, securing, and even storing your ribbon. I've also included a quick refresher course on the simple tools and supplies you'll need to make these handsome and imaginative projects.

Ribbon

RIBBON CLASSIFICATION

Ribbons are grouped into three main categories based on their manufacturing process. Each category's name tells how its ribbons are made.

CUT-EDGE RIBBONS
(also Craft Ribbons or Florist's Ribbons)

Cut-edge ribbons are made by cutting wide fabric into narrow strips. Imagine buying a yard of fabric, and then cutting it across its width into 1-inch (2.5 cm) strips. The cut fabric is then treated with a stiffening agent to add body and stability. The stiffening agent also prevents the cut fabric from fraying.

Cut-edge ribbons

Cut-edge ribbons, available in a variety of widths, are usually inexpensive. Many are printed with seasonal motifs. Most cut-edge ribbons can't be washed, but some can be dry-cleaned. They aren't appropriate for projects that will receive much handling, such as embellished wearables and bed and table linens. Always check the ribbon's spool for recommended care instructions.

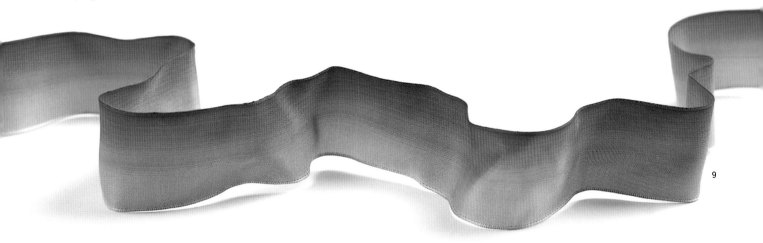

Woven-Edge Ribbons

Woven-edge ribbons aren't cut from larger fabric pieces. Their fibers are woven to the desired width in narrow strips with two selvage edges. Selvage, the finished edges on either side of a woven or flat-knitted fabric, prevents fraying. It's often a narrow border of different or heavier threads than the body of the ribbon, and sometimes it's a different fiber weave. Woven-edge ribbons can have both straight and decorative edges. Some even have a scalloped, or picot, finish. Many woven-edge ribbons are washable, colorfast, and shrink-resistant.

Picot-edge ribbons

Wire-Edge Ribbons

There are three principal ways of creating wire-edge ribbons: a fine wire can be woven directly into the fabric along the ribbon's edges; wire can be positioned at the ribbon's edge and overlocked by the fabric, forming a thin hem; or the ribbon itself can be made of delicate wire mesh with some additional silk or metallic fibers. You may even find a wire-edge ribbon that has an extra wire or wires woven through the middle of the fabric. Like the edge wires, these supplemental wires run the length of ribbon and help hold the ribbon's shape.

Wire-edge ribbons have great flexibility and durability. You can loop, bend, fold, or pleat them into any shape, and they'll hold their position indefinitely. They're also a very forgiving ribbon. If you aren't pleased with any twist or turn, you can straighten out the ribbon wires and begin again. If you're in the middle of a project and need to refer to the instructions, there's no need to keep grasping the ribbon or to secure it with pins. The wire keeps the ribbon in shape until you've sorted out the process. (This is particularly helpful when tying fancy gift bows.) The main drawback to crafting with wire-edge ribbons is that most cannot be washed.

Wire-edge ribbons

RIBBON FIBERS & TEXTURES

After being classified by their manufacturing process, ribbons are further grouped by their fibers, textures, and weaves. Ribbon fibers come from natural sources such as cotton, linen, and silk, and man-made synthetic materials such as polyester, nylon, and acrylic. A ribbon's texture and weave are its most distinguishing characteristics, allowing for easy categorization. Here are some notable types.

Grosgrain

In French, grosgrain means coarse texture, an accurate description of these ribbed, close-woven, very utilitarian ribbons. Although this name may be strange to you, it refers to one of the most common and familiar ribbons. Because of its exceptional durability, grosgrain ribbon has played an important role in many popular fashions. Traditionally grosgrain ribbons encircle the brim of bowler hats, are tied around pigtails, and plaited into braids. Grosgrain ribbons may be solid or patterned, and have straight or scalloped edges. Some showy grosgrain ribbons even have pleats. Grosgrain ribbons are often made from a blend of natural and synthetic fibers, usually cotton with viscose or polyester.

Grosgrain ribbons

Jacquard

This class of ribbon takes its name from Monsieur Joseph Marie Jacquard, an 18th-century French inventor. He developed the commercial loom that revolutionized the ribbon industry. Jacquard ribbons possess the most sophisticated designs. Their intricate weave resembles ornate tapestry. Traditional jacquards depict floral, animal, geometric, or ethnic motifs. Because of their high cost, most ribbon suppliers only carry a small stock. To find the best in new and vintage jacquards, search out specialty fabric stores and Internet retailers.

Vintage jacquard ribbon

Jacquard ribbons

Metallic

Shimmering metallic ribbons come in a luscious array of textures, patterns, and weaves. Although most closely associated with holiday celebrations and gift packaging, metallic ribbons make any ribbon project sparkle. Their luminosity primarily comes from the glow of their special threads, but is often enhanced by the translucence of a loose weave. Metallic ribbons are available with a cut, woven, or wire edge.

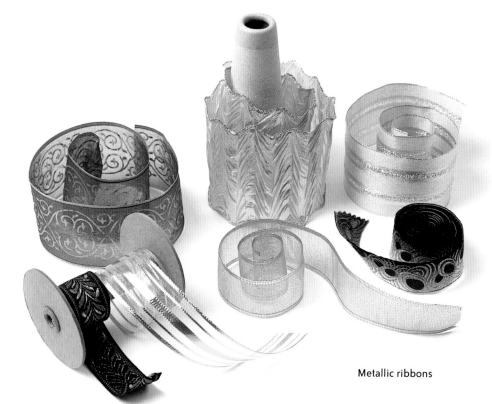

Metallic ribbons

Ombré

This painterly ribbon is characterized by colors or tones that gradually blend into each other across the ribbon's width. The term ombré primarily describes fabrics on which the color turns from light to dark. Ombré ribbons can be created from natural or synthetic fibers, have metallic thread inclusions, and wire edges. Some textile artists even hand-dye silks to create the ombré effect.

Ombré ribbons

Organdy

Very sheer and transparent, organdy is the most delicate ribbon. Originally silk, most organdy ribbon is now made from synthetic threads. Its airy appearance is often bordered by thicker woven or wired edges. Beyond plain sheers, organdy ribbons can include metallic fibers, be appliqued or embroidered, or have printed or woven designs. Distinctly romantic, organdy ribbons are the most popular choice for wedding ribbon crafts.

Organdy ribbons

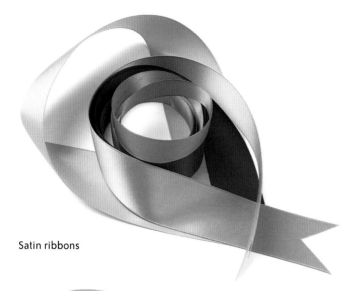

Satin ribbons

Satin

Satin ribbon is characterized by its unmistakable luster. This glossy deep sheen can appear on one or both sides of the ribbon. (Single-faced satin has a dull side, while double-faced satin does not.) Satin is produced by a specific weaving process. Its warp threads interlace with filling threads to produce a smooth-faced fabric. Available in almost every width imaginable, satin ribbons come in solid colors or woven or printed patterns. Their edges may be woven, wire, or picot.

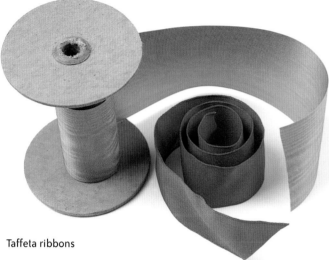

Taffeta ribbons

Taffeta

One of the oldest, most luxurious fabrics, taffeta is crisp with a subtle sheen. It's produced with fibers, such as silk or nylon, that are woven very close together. Taffeta ribbons are generally stiff and have a lot of body. Their surfaces also may have patterns such as moire, a rippled wavy finish, and sometimes include designs in metallic thread. Taffeta ribbons often have a woven, wired, or even jacquard edge. Their surfaces can be pleated or even flocked.

Velvet

Classic elegance is exemplified by the soft texture and rich saturated colors of velvet. Even as tiny bows, these ribbons dress up every item they adorn. Velvet ribbon has a distinctive pile on at least one side and sometimes both sides. (Single-pile velvet ribbons are often satin-backed.) Velvet's pile is produced by weaving an extra set of yarns that form raised loops. The loops are later cut and trimmed. Velvet ribbon surfaces are solid, patterned, or flocked. The ribbon edges may be straight, wire-edged, scalloped, or pleated.

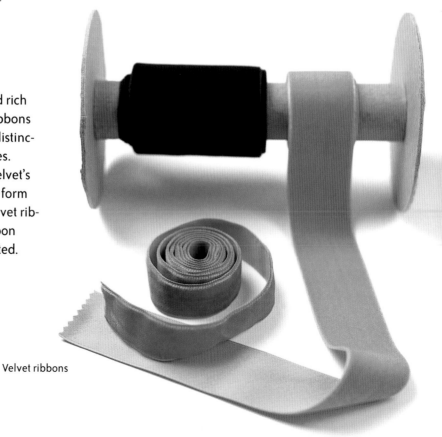

Velvet ribbons

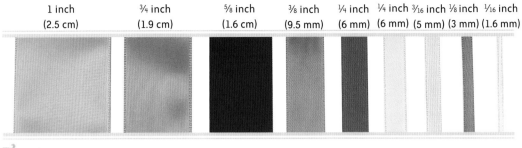

1 inch (2.5 cm)	¾ inch (1.9 cm)	⅝ inch (1.6 cm)	⅜ inch (9.5 mm)	¼ inch (6 mm)	¼ inch (6 mm)	³⁄₁₆ inch (5 mm)	⅛ inch (3 mm)	¹⁄₁₆ inch (1.6 mm)

RIBBON WIDTH

Ribbon widths range from delicate $\frac{1}{16}$-inch (1.6 mm) wisps of color to imposing 6-inch (15.2 cm) bands. The

Figure 1

width of the ribbon is often printed on the spool in both inches and millimeters. If the ribbon is being sold by the spool, its length also will be specified. The ribbon's fiber content, laundering instructions, and suggested uses may be included as well. To see a chart representing the diversity of ribbon widths, refer to figure 1.

Prepleated ribbon trim

PURCHASING RIBBON

Now that you are more fully attuned to the varieties of ribbon, your next visit to the fabric or craft supply store will be a real pleasure. You can now make informed decisions about the type of ribbon needed for your project. Beyond flat ribbons, you're likely to notice an ever-increasing variety of novelty products, such as ready-made flowers and bows, and prepleated trim. Some stores sell ribbon by the yard or meter, while others require you to purchase prepackaged lengths. Although you may be reluctant to buy a full spool because it's more ribbon that you need, don't let this stop you. Full spools often are the economical choice, and your leftovers might inspire future projects. Ribbon scraps also come in handy when you're wrapping gift packages. (What a relief not to have to run to the store at the last minute to purchase a bow!) The convenience of a well-stocked ribbon box puts plenty of choices at your fingertips.

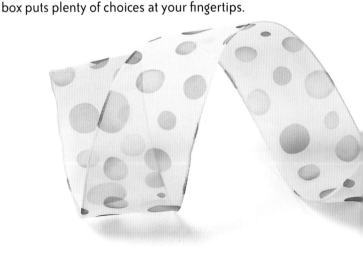

CHOOSING COLORS

Color preferences vary dramatically from person to person. You can see this reflected in a friend's wardrobe or a neighbor's home decor. Even family members hold strong opinions regarding color. I've taken this into account while writing this book. Although the width, length, and type of ribbon appears on a project's materials list, its color does not. If you'd like to recreate a particular design, the photos and parenthetical references provide that information. If you want to change the colors to express your personal taste or to please a friend's, go right ahead.

STORING RIBBON

Have you ever wondered why ribbon is wrapped around spools? Creases form in folded ribbons that are nearly impossible to remove. Rolling ribbons is an excellent conservation practice that prevents creases from forming. To make rolls, loop the ribbon around your fingers or a tube. Most wired ribbons maintain their shape. If the roll is not secure, bind it with a straight pin or paper clip. If using a tube, cut one diagonal slit at each end and insert the ends of the ribbon. Ideally you should store your rolled ribbons in a plastic, lidded box. Cardboard boxes, if not archival, contain chemicals that can damage your ribbons over time.

Supplies & Tools

You'll only need a few tools and supplies to make our simple ribbon crafts. In reviewing this basic information, you might pick up some valuable tips.

Clockwise from top left: hand-sewing needles, invisible thread, sewing thread, fabric scissors, small sewing scissors, fusible interfacing

SCISSORS

You simply can't have too many pairs of scissors. Whether you're wrapping a gift, creating a flower arrangement, or harvesting fresh herbs, it's comforting to know you've stashed a trusty set of blades nearby—but resist using these on ribbon. Instead, treat yourself to a set of fabric scissors. It's a small investment that ultimately will prove quite valuable. Use your fabric scissors solely on fabric and non-wire-edge ribbons. This will keep their blades sharp for precision cutting. Cut wire-edge ribbons with a sharp and clean pair of utility scissors. Also have a small pair of sewing scissors on hand to trim loose or frayed ribbon fibers from your project.

ADHESIVES

Craft glue, or PVA (polyvinyl acetate), is a common and well-loved fixative. It's very effective for bonding light materials. Simple to apply, PVA also quickly dries clear. For a reliable and enduring hold, PVA is the answer for most of your ribbon-gluing needs. For best results, pour a small amount of PVA into a shallow plastic container, and then use a stiff-bristled artist's paintbrush to evenly smooth the glue over the surface you're gluing. Lay your ribbon over the glue and gently apply pressure. Wipe away any excess glue with a paper towel or clean cloth. Let the glue dry completely before handling.

Some craft glues, especially those made specifically for fabric, boast higher flexibility when dry. Depending on your project, this may be an important attribute. You also may want to determine if the glue is washable and/or dry-cleanable before using. Due to the variety of ribbon fibers and applications, please remember to test glues on scrap samples before using.

You can use a hot glue gun and hot glue to adhere ribbon in some cases. Using a stiff-bristled artist's paintbrush to flatten and evenly distribute the hot glue helps keep the ribbon flat. Thick lines of glue can buckle the ribbon, produce a bumpy surface, and prevent a lasting bond.

FUSIBLES

If you like ribbon crafts but not sewing, fusible products provide a wonderful alternative. You'll be able to bond ribbons to fabrics or other ribbons without using a needle and thread. Fusibles permanently join two layers of fabric by melting between them under the heat and pressure of an iron, providing shape, support, and security. Fusibles provide crisp results and are an excellent choice for ribbons that fray. They come in a variety of sizes and weights, ranging from heavy interfacing sheets to light hem tape. Some ribbons, such as metallics, velvets, and open mesh, don't react well to fusibles. Fusibles can be a real time and labor saver, as long as you carefully follow the manufacturer's directions. To assure a good bond, always prewash the fabric you'll be fusing to get rid of finishing products or sizing. These agents inhibit proper fusing. Always test the fusible interfacing on a scrap of ribbon before you begin to be sure it works and that you like the results.

HAND-SEWING NEEDLES

The right type of needle makes a world of difference in the ease, appearance, and quality of your hand stitching. Keep a variety of needles with your sewing supplies. Needles are commonly numbered according to their size—the smaller the number, the longer and thicker the needle.

All-purpose hand-sewing needles, or sharps, have a medium length and small rounded eyes. For detailed handwork, you may want to choose a shorter needle, or a between, with a small rounded eye. Beading needles are very long and fine with a small, round eye. Use them to attach beads or small pearls. Use upholstery needles on thick, tightly woven upholstery fabrics. In the ever-expanding world of needles, there is even a self-threading variety good for users who have poorer eyesight.

THREADS

The three major categories of thread are based on fiber content. The first variety of thread comes from natural sources such as animals or plants. The most common animal fibers are silk, from the cocoons of the silkworm, and wool, from the fleece of sheep. Familiar plant fibers are cotton and linen. The second thread category covers those that come from man-made sources. These synthetic threads offer new opportunities for different textures and effects. The final type of threads are blends of more than one fiber. They can be anything from a mix of silk and wool to blends of man-made fibers.

Threads come in a wide range of weights and colors. Some are twisted and must be used as one thread, while others are made up of several strands which can be separated and used singly or put together in different weight and color combinations. It's important to select an appropriate thread for the sewing technique you're using. For decorative stitching, you may want to use a different type of thread than that used for basic hand- and machine-sewing. This opens up yet another world of exciting creative discovery.

SEWING MACHINE

Ribbon crafters can use any sewing machine in good working order. Read the detailed user's guide published by your machine's manufacturer to learn practical information such as threading, winding bobbins, using accessories, and controlling tension. You can create original works of art on a standard sewing machine, so explore its decorative possibilities, too. One of them might turn out to be just the right technique for your next project.

Use the right sewing machine needles for your project, making sure they're sharp and straight. The correct machine-needle size is determined by the weight of the fabric and/or ribbon to be sewn. Usually heavier-weight fabrics are best sewn with larger needles. Select the type of thread you prefer (generally cotton or polyester), making sure it suits the job and the needle. Although most often the thread size is the same for the bobbin and the needle, you may want to experiment with variations. Using different thread weights sometimes yields fascinating effects. Give plenty of consideration to the color of the thread. Do you want the thread to be invisible, to match the ribbon, to complement the ribbon's tones, or to stand out in sharp contrast?

17

FRAY RETARDANT

This liquid adhesive stops the threads on cut ribbon edges from fraying or unraveling. Fray retardants won't stain or stiffen your ribbon, and most dry immediately. The most popular varieties of fray retardant are washable and dry cleanable, but always check the printed label for care instructions.

MARKERS

Several types of fabric markers are useful to ribbon crafters. Dressmaker's pens make marks on fabric that can be removed with water or a fabric eraser. Some air-soluble inks disappear over time.

ODDS & ENDS

Although ribbons are perfectly glorious on their own, some projects may need a little extra embellishment. You'll find it useful to maintain a stash of interesting odds and ends just for this purpose. Keep a box of beads, charms, costume jewelry, fabric scraps, patches, lace, leaves, trims, feathers, flowers, miniatures, or anything else that strikes your fancy. Creative inspiration often comes from such treasure troves.

A variety of ribbon craft embellishments

Techniques

Step-by-step directions thoroughly explain the techniques used to create each project. Here are some extra tips for working with ribbon.

RIBBON TIPS

• Buy a little more ribbon that you think you need; 12 inches (30.5 cm) extra is sufficient. This overage covers your seam allowance and allows you to neaten the ends of the ribbon.

• If you alter a project or create one of your own, sketch your design on paper. This helps you determine how much ribbon to buy.

• It's possible and quite easy to remove the wires from some wire-edge ribbons. Push out the tip of the wire from one edge of the ribbon. Firmly grasp the wire with your fingers or a pair of tweezers, and gently pull it out. As needed, push down the ribbon, bunching it up along the edge to expose more wire. Cut off the wire as needed.

• When machine-stitching ribbon, sew in the same direction on both edges. This prevents the ribbon from puckering.

• If you have to sew many adjoining ribbons, consider first fusing them to a sheet of lightweight interfacing.

• Many people like the look of fork-cut ribbon ends (figure 2a), but few know how simply they can be perfected. To make the cut, fold your ribbon in half lengthwise (figure 2b); then diagonally cut the end of the ribbon from the corner points to the folded edge (figure 2c).

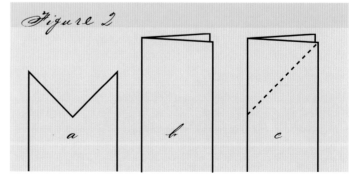

EASY RIBBON FLOWER TECHNIQUES

Several projects, such as the Summer Sun Hat on page 78, the Pin Pillow on page 93, and the Drawstring Purse on page 118, use ribbon roses and other flowers in a contemporary way. Refer to this standard set of instructions when making these projects. Use these or any other favored flower techniques to make the embellishment you desire.

Wired Ribbon Rose

1. Make a knot at one end of a length of wired ribbon (figure 3a).

2. Gently pull out one wire from the opposite ribbon end, as shown in figure 3b. Carefully and evenly gather the ribbon as you pull more and more wire. Do not cut off the wire.

3. While holding the knotted ribbon end in one hand, curl the gathered ribbon around the knot with your other hand. First tightly coil the ribbon to form the rose's bud, and then loosely coil the ribbon to create the open petals.

4. Fold down the cut ribbon end to the base of the rose, as shown in figure 3c.

5. Tightly wrap the wire around the knotted ribbon and the loose cut ribbon ends to secure (figure 3d). Cut off excess wire.

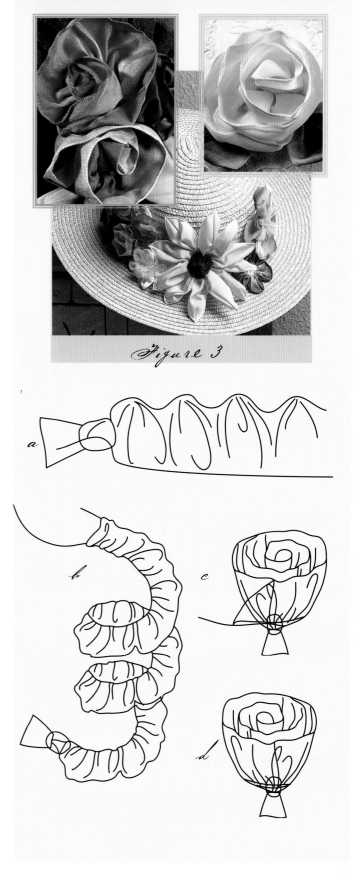

Figure 3

Leaf

1. Cut a length of ribbon. Fold each end diagonally to the center point of the ribbon (figure 4a). Fold each side towards center again to form a point.

2. There are two ways to secure the leaf. You can sew a gathering stitch along the bottom ends of the ribbon (figure 4b), pull the stitch to gather the ribbon, and tie off the thread. Or, you can gather the bottom ends of the ribbon and wrap them with wire (figure 4c) or bind them with a bit of hot glue.

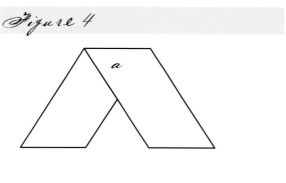

Pointed Flower Petals

1. Cut a length of ribbon and fold it in half, overlapping its ends (figure 5a).

2. Sew a gathering stitch across the overlapped ribbon ends (figure 5b).

3. Gently pull the thread to tightly gather the flower petal. Wrap the excess thread around the gathered end. Knot, and then trim the thread if making a single petal. If making a chain of pointed petals, as in the case of a sunflower, don't trim the thread. Repeat steps 1 through 3 to add additional petals (figure 5c and 5d).

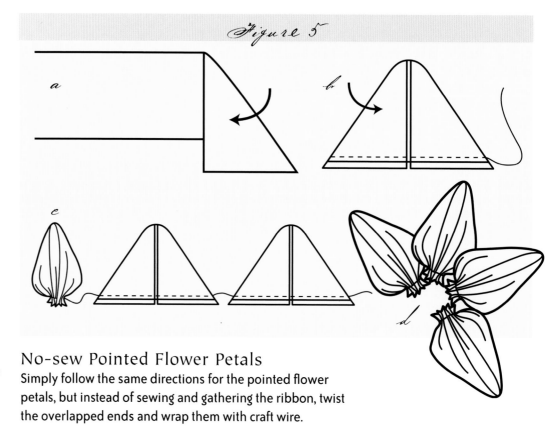

No-sew Pointed Flower Petals

Simply follow the same directions for the pointed flower petals, but instead of sewing and gathering the ribbon, twist the overlapped ends and wrap them with craft wire.

20

The
Maypole

Many mystic legends surround this rite of spring. The maypole is most commonly understood to be a pagan symbol of fertility. Ceremonial dances performed around the maypole were believed to assure the prosperity of the land and its people. Ribbons of many colors were intertwined around the maypole by young women dancing in a highly choreographed fashion. Each village danced a unique step, resulting in a distinct ribbon weave. Often there were several rings of dancers. The youngest girls danced simple patterns closest to the maypole, while the eldest took the outer ring and danced the most complex pattern. It was believed that if the ribbons were beautifully woven without breaking, the village would be rewarded with good fortune.

The Projects

Our ribbon crafts give you the opportunity

to express yourself with taste and style. Some

projects showcase a lot of ribbon while others

feature just a small ribbon accent. Whether you're

looking for fresh home decorating concepts,

stylish wearables and accessories, gift giving and

wrapping ideas, or heirlooms to treasure, you'll

find designs that will delight and inspire you.

No-Sew Chic Napkin Rings

Create these napkin rings in a flash for a dinner party, family meal, or as a super-special housewarming gift. Here's the perfect opportunity to make a truly unique artistic statement by mixing and matching different ribbon colors and patterns.

WHAT YOU NEED

Solid-color grosgrain ribbons, 1¹⁄₂ inches (3.8 cm) wide

1 or 2 cardboard tubes (paper towel tube, etc.)

Measuring tape

Patterned woven-edge ribbons, 1 inch (2.5 cm) wide

Fusible webbing and fabric glue, or hand-sewing needle and thread

Small rubber bands

What You Do

1. Wrap the end of one solid grosgrain ribbon around the cardboard tube. Mark the overlap, and then cut the ribbon to this length. Use the measuring tape to determine the length of the cut ribbon. Cut the remaining solid grosgrain ribbons to this measurement.

2. Cut pieces of the patterned woven-edge ribbons the same length as the grosgrain ribbons cut in step 1. Cut the same number of pieces.

3. Following the manufacturer's instructions, use the fusible webbing to adhere the patterned ribbon to the center of the grosgrain ribbon. Alternate the colors and patterns to create an interesting set of rings.

4. One at a time, wrap the grosgrain ribbons around the cardboard tube. Secure the ends of the ribbon to each other with fabric glue; then put a rubber band around the ribbon to hold it in place until the glue is dry. Alternately, you can forego the fusible webbing and fabric glue and simply stitch the ribbons with a hand-sewing needle and thread.

Zesty Mosaic Tray

Drinks served on this vibrant tray may taste even more refreshing. The frame can be painted any color of the rainbow, so let your creative spirit soar. This is a great opportunity to use cherished scraps of ribbon you knew better than to discard.

WHAT YOU NEED

11 x 14-inch (27.9 x 35.6 cm) unfinished wood frame with glass and backing

Primer

Paintbrush

Black spray paint, or other color

Assorted pieces of ribbon

11 x 14-inch (27.9 x 35.6 cm) piece of white watercolor paper

Fabric glue

2 decorative handles with hardware

Drill

Screwdriver

4 wood craft balls, or decorative knobs

Wood glue

What You Do

1. Disassemble the frame, removing the glass and backing. Paint the primer on the wood to cover. Let dry. Spray paint the frame, using thin even coats. Let dry.

2. Cut the assorted ribbons to desired shapes and sizes. Arrange the ribbon pieces on top of the glass in a pleasing pattern.

3. Following the pattern created in step 2, use the fabric glue to adhere the ribbon pieces to the watercolor paper.

4. Measure and mark the position for the decorative handles on the underside of the frame. (The handles on this tray are centered on the short sides.) Drill pilot holes for the hardware at these points. Use a screwdriver and the supplied hardware to attach the handles to the tray.

5. Assemble the glass, the ribbon-mosaic paper, and backing, and then place them into the frame.

6. Prime and spray paint the wood craft balls (or decorative knobs) as desired. Let dry. Use wood glue or screws to attach these feet to the underside of the frame.

DESIGNER

JOAN K. MORRIS

Sheer *Bliss*

Glorious fern silhouettes are so naturally beautiful that all they need is a clever display to become an important part of your home decor. Can you find the ribbons here? They're wide enough to be used as the pockets.

2½ yards (2.3 m) sheer ribbon, 5 inches (12.7 cm) wide (white)

Iron and ironing board

Sewing machine

Invisible thread

White sheer curtain

11 dried or silk fern leaves

What You Do

1. Measure and cut 11 pieces of the sheer ribbon, each 7 inches (17.8 cm) long. If the ribbon is wired, remove the wires from both edges.

2. Fold down each cut ribbon edge to form a ¼-inch (6 mm) hem, and iron in place. Machine-stitch both hems with invisible thread.

3. Hang the sheer curtain so you can see its whole length. Pin the ribbon pockets onto the sheer, randomly placing them into a pleasing pattern. Make sure all pockets are level.

4. Machine-stitch each pocket, sewing close to the edge. Start at the upper left corner and carefully sew around to the upper right corner.

5. Once all 11 pockets are stitched to the shade, place one dried or silk fern leaf into each pocket.

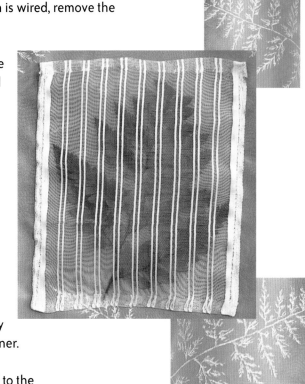

DESIGNER

JEN HAMILTON

Sun, Sand & Sea Tote

Hot, hot, hot! These vibrant ribbons reflect the spirit of the season, setting the perfect mood for a day at the beach. The bag is the perfect size to hold a towel, flip-flops, sunscreen, and a water bottle. A simple weave of ribbons is all it takes to make a plain tote into a stylish accessory.

Plastic tote bag with gaps for weaving

Measuring tape

Assorted woven-edge ribbons of the same width, in bright sunny tones

Fabric glue or fray retardant

What You Do

1. Measure the circumference and the height of the bag. Cut one ribbon the length of the bag's circumference. Measure the width of the cut ribbon. Divide the height of the bag by the width of the cut ribbon. The number you come up with is the minimum number of ribbons needed to fill the height of your bag. Measure and cut all ribbons.

2. Weave each ribbon in and out through the gaps in the plastic tote bag. If you wish to create additional embellishments, you can tie bows at various points on the bag.

3. Apply fabric glue or fray retardant to the cut ends of the ribbons to prevent fraying.

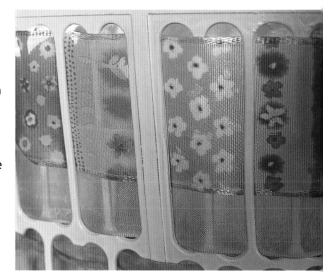

Versatile Orbs

Let your imagination (and design style) guide your approach to creating these attractive interior accents. Dress up your orbs in velvet for an elegant dining room centerpiece, or follow our lead and cover the balls in casual burlap. This project is a great way to show off small lengths of fantastic ribbon.

2 polystyrene balls, 3 inches (7.6 cm) in diameter

2 polystyrene balls, 4 inches (10.2 cm) in diameter

2 photocopied patterns, on this page

4 squares of burlap fabric, each 5 x 5 inches (12.7 x 12.7 cm), for 3-inch (7.6 cm) balls

4 squares of burlap fabric, each 6 x 6 inches (15.2 x 15.2 cm), for 4-inch (10.2 cm) balls

Straight pins

Hot glue gun and fabric glue sticks

Floral picks, optional

Assorted ribbons, each at least 6 inches (15.2 cm) long, various colors, patterns, and textures

Upholstery tacks

Decorative bowl

What You Do

1. Pick one size ball to cover first. Cut out the appropriate photocopied pattern for the ball and pin it to the appropriately sized burlap square. Cut out the burlap following the pattern lines, and then remove the paper. Repeat to make a second piece of trimmed burlap.

2. Lay both pieces of burlap fabric over the ball and determine out how to fit them together for gluing. (Each ball requires two pieces of burlap.) Make any additional cuts necessary to get the fabric to lay flat on the ball.

3. Little by little, glue the fabric to the ball with the hot glue gun until the whole ball is covered. Work with the fabric to make it as flat as possible. (You can further secure the fabric with a floral pick by placing it over the desired area and pushing it until the pick is flush with the ball's surface.)

4. Arrange the ribbons to go around the ball in a pleasing design. Cut the ribbons as needed to form spherical or elliptical rings. Use the hot glue gun to adhere the ribbons to the burlap covered ball. Work slowly and press the ribbon flat to hold. After all desired ribbons are applied, let the glue dry.

5. Push upholstery tacks in the top, sides, or bottom of the ball as desired. The tacks work especially well in places where there are multiple ribbon layers.

6. Cover and decorate a few more balls of varying sizes, and then place them in an attractive bowl.

Enlarge pattern to 150% for 3-inch (7.6 cm) ball. Enlarge pattern to 200% for 4-inch (10.2 cm) ball.

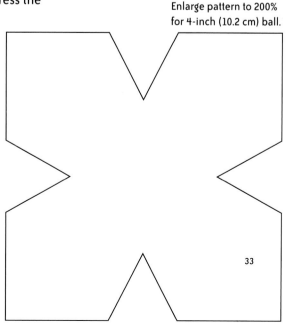

33

DESIGNERS
ALLISON SMITH & TERRY TAYLOR

Button & Bow Candle

*Give organza ribbon
and button flowers an
unexpected, contemporary
twist by displaying them
on brightly colored,
angular candles. Plant
a garden of several candles
on a small tray—
the more, the merrier.*

WHAT YOU NEED

5 yards (4.5 m) of white organza ribbon, ¼ inch (6 mm) wide

Hot glue gun and glue sticks

Pillar candles

20 to 25 small buttons in a mixed assortment of four colors

What You Do

1. Measure and cut a 10-inch (25.4 cm) length of the organza ribbon.

2. Squeeze a small amount of hot glue on the candle. Press the end of the short length of ribbon on the candle. Work quickly using a figure-eight motion to form five ribbon petals, each about 1 inch (2.5 cm) long. Use additional glue to secure the loops if needed.

3. Create as many ribbon flowers on the large candle as you wish. Don't place the flowers too near the wick.

4. Use a small amount of hot glue to attach a button to the center of each ribbon flower. Don't worry about the glue squeezing up through the holes in each button; it makes an unusual stamen for your ribbon flower.

DESIGNER
JULIE BELL

Beaded Bookmark

Here's an easy project that combines the beauty of ribbons and beads. Feel free to adapt the beaded shape, string a collection of unusual beads, or select any ribbon that suits your fancy. Ribbon bookmarks last longer than paper ones, and these take on special meaning because they're made by hand.

Assorted small glass beads

24-gauge wire

Silver end cap beads

Wire cutters

14 inches (35.6 cm) of grosgrain ribbon, 1 inch (2.5 cm) wide

Iron

Hand-sewing needle and thread

What You Do

1. String approximately 8 inches (20.3 cm) of small glass beads onto the 24-gauge wire. Add and secure a silver end cap bead to one end of the wire. Leave the other end of the wire undone. (Later, when shaping the wire into the desired letter, you'll need room to move the beads around.)

2. Decide what letter or shape you want the beaded wire to take (in the photo, it's the letter B). Bend the wire to make the desired shape, and then twist it to secure. Cut off the end of the wire once you've made your shape, and tie on a silver end cap bead.

3. Fold one end of the ribbon ¼ inch (6 mm) under, and then ¼ inch (6 mm) under again. Iron the fold to create a neat hem.

4. Slide the beaded wire through the hem. To secure the beaded wire, use a needle and thread to sew small stitches across the ribbon.

5. Fold the other end of the ribbon ¼ inch (6 mm) under, and then ¼ inch (6 mm) under again. Iron the fold to make a neat hem. You could put another beaded wire shape in the hem and sew it closed, or sew a few random beads on the hem to finish.

DESIGNER
MARVIS A. LUTZ

Beautiful Borders

The simple application of ribbon trim adds a distinctive flourish to your wardrobe and your children's. Many jacquard ribbons have delightful woven designs. These polar fleece jackets are embellished with a very fitting Nordic-inspired pattern.

What You Do

Item of clothing to be embellished

Measuring tape

Jacquard ribbon in any width, long enough to cover desired areas plus a little extra

Straight pins

Hand-sewing needle or sewing machine

Hand-sewing thread

1. Measure the area to be trimmed with ribbon and add 1 or 2 inches (2.5 or 5 cm). Cut a length of ribbon to this measurement.

2. Use straight pins to attach the ribbon onto the clothing in the desired location.

3. Hand- or machine-stitch one edge of the ribbon to the fabric. Turn under a ¼- to ½-inch (6 mm to 1.3 cm) hem at each end. Sew the second edge to the fabric, working in the same direction and matching the hems. Remove the straight pins.

4. Repeat steps 1 through 3 for each piece of ribbon you wish to apply to the clothing.

DESIGNER
JEN HAMILTON

Supernova Shade

This galaxy of ribbons strung with moons and stars lends a cosmic touch to any window. Select ribbons that appeal to you—sheer and opaque, textured and smooth, skinny and thick—all varieties will do. Painting and stringing the ornaments is an activity the whole family can enjoy.

WHAT YOU NEED

Approximately 11 yards
(10 m) of ribbon in
various colors, widths,
and textures

33-inch (83.8 cm) wood
dowel rod, 1 inch
(2.5 cm) in diameter

2 wood craft balls,
1½ inches (3.8 cm) in
diameter

¾-inch (1.9 cm)
wooden beads,
approximately 19

Assorted wooden
ornaments,
approximately 10

Acrylic paints in shades
to match ribbon

Paintbrush

Hand-sewing needle

Invisible thread

Wood glue

What You Do

1. Determine your ribbon design by laying the ribbons in a row and making adjustments. Measure and cut the ribbons in a random arrangement of 1-yard (.9 m), 2-foot (61 cm), and 1½-foot (45.7 cm) lengths.

2. Paint the wood dowel and craft balls with different colors of acrylic paint. Paint the wooden beads and ornaments with the acrylic paints. Paint the edges of the ornaments a contrasting color if desired. Let all painted surfaces dry completely.

3. To hang a painted ornament, thread one end of a ribbon through its hole and secure it with a knot. Thread the opposite ribbon end through a painted bead, and slide the bead down the ribbon to cover the knot.

4. To hang a single bead, tie a knot at one end of the ribbon, thread the other end through the bead, and then slide it down the ribbon to the knot.

5. On the loose end of each ribbon, make a hanging loop large enough to fit over the painted wood dowel and easily slide along its length. Use a needle and invisible thread to hand-sew the loop closed.

6. Slide each loop over the dowel in the order you arranged in step 1. Use the wood glue to adhere the painted balls onto the ends of the dowel.

Chopstick Pocket

Sew this simple chopstick case, and then decorate your table with a distinctly Asian

flair. The red raw-silk ribbon is wide enough to use as fabric—just fold and stitch.

Embellish the pocket with a simple linoleum block print if you like. In Japanese,

this particular symbol means "to eat," and with such an inviting presentation,

who could resist?

WHAT YOU NEED

Photocopied design template, on this page*

Vellum or tracing paper*

Linoleum block*

Linoleum cutter*

Block-printing ink for fabric*

Brayer*

Cotton fabric, at least 5 x 5 inches (12.7 x 12.7 cm) square

12 inches (30.5 cm) satin ribbon, ¼ inch (6 mm) wide

Fabric glue

15 inches (38.1 cm) silk ribbon, 2⅝ inches (6.6 cm) wide

Hand-sewing thread

*You can omit these materials and skip steps 1 through 3 by purchasing a commercial rubber stamp and ink block or by using printed fabric.

What You Do *

1. Trace the photocopied template onto a piece of vellum or tracing paper. Lay the tracing paper on top of the linoleum block, image side down. Rub the back of the paper with a blunt tool, such as the back of a spoon or your fingernail, to burnish the pencil markings onto the carving block. Lift the paper to make sure the image completely transferred. Pencil in any missed areas.

2. Using the linoleum cutter, gently carve away the area of the block that makes up the background to the design. You will end up with a raised Japanese character, or *Kanji*, that is the mirror image of the original.

3. Pour a small amount of block-printing ink into a shallow container, such as a plastic lid. Evenly roll a thin layer of ink onto the brayer. Press the carved and inked block onto the cotton fabric. Once the ink is dry, mark a 2 x 2-inch (5 x 5 cm) square around the print and cut it out.

4. Cut four 2-inch (5 cm) lengths of the ¼-inch-wide (6 mm) satin ribbon, one for each edge of the stamped cotton fabric. Adhere the side ribbon pieces to the stamped fabric with the fabric glue. Adhere the top and bottom ribbon pieces, gluing their ends over the ends of the side pieces. Let dry.

5. Turn a ½-inch (1.3 cm) hem at both ends of the 2 ⅝-inch-wide (6.6 cm) silk ribbon. Fold the hems in opposite directions (one under, one up). Fold and press or pin as needed to secure, and then hem both ends with a needle and thread.

6. Sew the ribbon-trimmed printed fabric square onto one end of the wide ribbon.

7. Fold the ribbon into two parts: one length measuring 8 inches (20.3 cm) and the other, 6 inches (15.2 cm). Sew up the sides of the ribbon to create the pocket for the chopstick holder.

24-Karat Bow

Top off your wedding or anniversary gift with a luxurious bow. This ornate embellishment is created from a single piece of ribbon. Its metallic diamond design beautifully complements the subtle argyle of the wrapping paper.

WHAT YOU NEED

3 yards (2.7 m) wire-edge ribbon, 2½ inches (6.4 cm) wide

Floral wire

What You Do

1. Make a loop on one end of the ribbon, leaving a tail equal to the length of the first loop. Keeping the ribbon pinched firmly between your thumb and forefinger, gather in the sides of the ribbon at the base of the loop.

2. Make a second loop of ribbon equal in size to the first loop. Place it on the opposite side of your thumb. Twist the ribbon as needed to keep the right side showing. Firmly pinch the ribbon between your thumb and forefinger as you gather the sides at the base of the loop.

3. Continue making equal-size loops until you have a total of six, all gathered between your thumb and forefinger.

4. Twisting the ribbon to show the right side, create a smaller loop on top of the first loop made in step 1.

5. Make five more smaller loops, placing one on top of each larger loop, until you have a total of six small loops.

6. Leave a tail on the ribbon equal to that left in step 1.

7. Wrap the floral wire around the center of the bow, bringing the ends of the wire behind the bow. Firmly twist the free ends of the wire to secure the bow.

8. Make a fork cut in each ribbon tail (see page 18 for directions).

Azure Fields BOW

Adorned with this professional-looking bow, your gift package will stand out from all the rest. Flat-style bows are great for displaying today's terrific ribbons, such as this sheer floral design. A series of seemingly complicated stacked loops, this bow is simpler to make than it appears.

1½ yards (1.4 m)
wire-edge ribbon,
2½ inches
(6.4 cm) wide

Floral wire

What You Do

1. Cut one piece of the wire-edge ribbon at each of the following four lengths: 18 inches (45.7 cm), 16 inches (40.6 cm), 12 inches (30.5 cm), and 7 inches (17.8 cm).

2. Make a fork cut at both ends of the 12-inch (30.5 cm) ribbon length (see page 18 for directions).

3. Make a single large loop out of the 18-inch (45.7 cm) piece of ribbon, overlapping the ends approximately 1½ inches (3.8 cm).

4. Center the seam of the looped ribbon on top of the 12-inch (30.5 cm) length of ribbon.

5. Make a single large loop out of the 16-inch (40.6 cm) piece of ribbon, overlapping the ends approximately 1½ inches (3.8 cm). Center the seam of this looped ribbon on top of the looped 18-inch (45.7 cm) ribbon.

6. Make a small loop with the 7-inch (17.8 cm) piece of ribbon, overlapping the ends, and place it in the center of the 16-inch (40.6 cm) looped ribbon.

7. Insert a piece of floral wire through the center loop, bringing both ends of the wire to the back of the bow. Tightly twist the wire to secure the bow.

DESIGNER
ALLISON SMITH

Woven Picture Frame

Create a fabulous contemporary frame by weaving together ribbons of complementary or contrasting colors. Use organza ribbon if you wish to create a sheer effect.

WHAT YOU NEED

Flat wooden frame, any size (the wider the borders, the better)

Ruler

2 ribbons of different colors

Hot glue gun and glue sticks

Poster board

Spray adhesive

12 x 12-inch (30.5 x 30.5 cm) scrap of fabric

What You Do

1. Measure the width and height of the frame. Add 2 inches (5 cm) to the height, and cut enough ribbon to line up edge to edge across the top of the frame. For example, if the frame is 5 inches (12.7 cm) wide and your ribbon is ½ inch (1.3 cm) wide, you'll need to cut 10 ribbons. Remember that the ribbons in the center of the frame need to be only half as long.

2. Cut the ribbons that will be woven horizontally following the method described in step 1.

3. Use hot glue to attach the ends of the ribbons to the top back side of the frame. Alternate colors as you go along, and keep the edges of the ribbon as close together as you can without overlapping.

4. Starting at the top of the frame, attach the first horizontal ribbon to the top left side of the frame. (Remember to attach the ribbon to the back of the frame.)

5. Weave the ribbon in and out of the ribbons hanging down from the top, and secure it on the back of the right side of the frame with hot glue.

6. Continue weaving with alternating ribbons. Be sure to keep the edges straight and close together. As you continue weaving, gently pull the vertical ribbons to keep them straight and flat.

7. When weaving the short side edges of the frame, simply weave to the center opening, secure the ribbon on the back inside center of

the frame with hot glue, and trim the ribbon. Secure the remaining ribbon on the opposite edge with hot glue, and continue weaving. Attach the end of the ribbon on the right side of the frame with hot glue.

8. To conceal the back of the frame, trace the frame onto the piece of poster board. Cut out the shape and trim the edges so they don't stick out around the edges of the frame. Spray with adhesive and cover with fabric. Wrap the edges around the poster board to make a clean edge. Attach to the back of the frame with hot glue in order to conceal the raw edges of the ribbon.

Buttercup & Gingham Linens

This cheerful sheet and pillowcase set has a look that is fresh as spring. The classic charm of the black-and-white gingham ribbon suits any bedroom, whether it's in a rustic cabin or a city high-rise. With basic machine-sewing skills, you'll be able to personalize your linens in an single afternoon.

WHAT YOU NEED

3½ yards (3.2 m) ribbon,
1 ½ inches (3.8 cm) wide
(thick gingham)

3½ yards (3.2 m) ribbon,
1 inch (2.5 cm) wide
(contrasting picot edge)

3½ yards (3.2 m) ribbon,
⅛ inch (3 mm) wide
(yellow)

4 yards (3.7 m) ribbon,
⅜ inch (9.5 mm) wide
(thin gingham)

Tape measure

**Prewashed twin-sized
flat sheet***

Straight pins

Sewing machine

Invisible thread

**Prewashed standard
pillowcase***

Hand-sewing needle

White sewing thread

*Larger sheets or pillowcas-
es require more ribbon, so
be sure to calculate the
additional amounts.

What You Do

1. Measure and cut a 2-yard (1.8 m) length of each of the ribbon varieties.

2. Measure 3 inches (7.6 cm) down from the top edge of the sheet's top left corner. Place the top edge of the 1½-inch-wide (3.8 cm) ribbon (gingham) at this point. Position the cut edge of the ribbon ½ inch (1.3 cm) past the sheet's left edge so it can be folded under. Pin the ribbon in place, and then work your way across the sheet continuing to pin the ribbon. Once you reach the sheet's right edge, leave another ½ inch (1.3 cm) of ribbon to fold under. Machine-stitch both edges of the ribbon in place with the invisible thread.

3. Pin the 2-yard (1.8 m) piece of ⅛-inch-wide (3 mm) ribbon (yellow) in the center of the ribbon sewn in step 2. Leave an extra ½ inch (1.3 cm) of ribbon on both sides of the sheet's edge to be turned under. Machine-stitch down the center of the ribbon with the invisible thread.

4. Following the method described in step 2, position the 2-yard (1.8 m) piece of 1-inch-wide (2.5 cm) ribbon (picot edge) 1½ inches (3.8

cm) in from the top edge of the sheet. Machine-stitch in place.

5. Following the method described in step 3, position the 2-yard (1.8 m) piece of ⅜-inch-wide (9.5 mm) ribbon (gingham) in the center of the 1-inch-wide (2.5 cm) ribbon (picot edge). Machine-stitch in place.

6. Measure 3 inches (7.6 cm) in from the edge of the pillowcase opening at its seam. Place the top edge of the remaining 1½ yards (1.4 m) of 1½-inch-wide (3.8 cm) ribbon (gingham) at this point, leaving a 1-inch (2.5 cm) length from the cut edge. Pin the ribbon all the way around the pillowcase. When you reach its seam, trim the ribbon, and fold under the extra 1 inch (2.5 cm) to cover the cut edge. Use the invisible thread to machine-stitch both edges of the ribbon in place.

7. Pin the remaining 1½ yards (1.4 m) of the ⅛-inch-wide (3 mm) ribbon (yellow) in the center of the ribbon sewn in step 6. As in step 6, leave 1 inch (2.5 cm) of ribbon at the starting edge to fold over and cover the cut edges. Machine-stitch in place.

8. Following the process described in step 6, place the remaining 1½ yards (1.4 m) of the 1-inch-wide (2.5 cm) ribbon (picot edge) 2 inches (5 cm) in from the edge of the pillowcase open-ing. Machine-stitch both edges in place.

9. With the remaining 2 yards (1.8 m) of the ⅜-inch-wide (9.5 mm) ribbon (gingham), you'll make a string of five bows. Measure 3 inches (7.6 cm) in from one end of the ribbon, and tie a 3-inch-wide (7.6 cm) bow. Measure 5 inches (12.7 cm) from this bow, and tie anoth-er. Repeat this process until you have a total of five bows.

10. Place the center bow in the middle of the 1-inch-wide (2.5 cm) ribbon (picot edge) and center it on the pillowcase. Make sure the tails of the ribbons face the pillowcase opening. Evenly arrange the remaining bows on either side of the center. Hand-stitch the bows in place.

11. Pull each ribbon tail toward the pillowcase open-ing, centering it between the bows, and hand-stitch in place.

DESIGNER

JOAN K. MORRIS

Rosy Ruffled Shade

A plain window shade dressed up with a surface of ribbons gives any room a designer touch. Mix and match sheer ribbons of any color, pattern, or width to create the look you desire. A simple ruffled edge and looped pull make the perfect finish.

WHAT YOU NEED

1½ yards (1.4 m) sheer ribbon, 2½ inches (6.4 cm) wide (polka dot)

2¾ yards (2.5 m) sheer ribbon, 2½ inches (6.4 cm) wide (floral on pink)

1½ yards (1.4 m) sheer ribbon, 1½ inches (3.8 cm) wide (pink-and-white stripe)

1½ yards (1.4 m) sheer ribbon, 1½ inches (3.8 cm) wide (floral on white)

1¼ yards (1.1 m) sheer ribbon, 2½ inches (6.4 cm) wide (pink-and-white stripe)

1¼ yards (1.1 m) sheer ribbon, 1½ inches (3.8 cm) wide (floral on pink)

1¼ yards (1.1 m) sheer ribbon, 1½ inches (3.8 cm) wide (polka dot)

Rolling window shade, 36 inches (.9 m) wide

Fabric glue

2 yards (1.8 m) wire-edge sheer ribbon, 2½ inches (6.4 cm) wide (floral on white)

Hot glue gun and glue stick

1. Measure and cut one 50-inch (1.3 m) length of the following ribbons: the 2½-inch-wide sheer ribbon (polka dot); the 2½-inch-wide sheer ribbon (floral on pink); the 1½-inch-wide sheer ribbon (pink-and-white stripe); and the 1½-inch-wide sheer ribbon (floral on white).

2. Measure and cut one 38-inch (.97 m) length of the following ribbons: the 2½-inch-wide sheer ribbon (pink-and-white stripe); the 2½-inch-wide sheer ribbon (floral on pink); the 1½-inch-wide sheer ribbon (floral on pink); and the 1½-inch-wide sheer ribbon (polka dot).

3. Measure and cut one 8-inch (20.3 cm) length of the 1½-inch-wide sheer ribbon (pink-and-white stripe) to use for the shade pull.

4. Unroll the window shade on top of a large table or flat work area. Lay out the four 50-inch (1.3 m) ribbons vertically on the shade. Place the 2½-inch-wide sheer ribbon (polka dot) 2 inches (5 cm) in from the right edge of the shade. Measure 2 inches (5 cm) to the left of the first ribbon, and position the 2½-inch-wide sheer ribbon (floral on pink). Measure another 2 inches (5 cm) to the left, and position the 1½-inch-wide sheer ribbon (floral on white). Measure another 2 inches (5 cm) to the left, and position the 1½-inch-wide sheer ribbon (pink-and-white stripe).

5. Starting 3 inches (7.6 cm) in from the bottom edge of the shade, leaving a 2-inch (5 cm) space between each ribbon, and 1 inch (2.5 cm) of ribbon hanging over each shade edge, lay out the four 38-inch (.96 m) ribbons horizontally in the following order (bottom to top): the 2½-inch-wide sheer ribbon (pink-and-white stripe); the 2½-inch-wide sheer ribbon (floral on pink); the 1½-inch-wide sheer ribbon (floral on pink); and the 1½-inch-wide sheer ribbon (polka dot).

6. Following the manufacturer's directions, use the fabric glue to adhere each ribbon. Since this type of glue dries slowly, you'll have plenty of time to arrange the ribbons. In the lower right corner of the shade, where the ribbons intersect, you can weave the ribbons in a simple over-and-under pattern if desired.

7. Fold the extra 1 inch (2.5 cm) of ribbon found at each end of each horizontal ribbon to the underside of the shade, and glue in place. Let the fabric glue completely dry.

8. Remove the wire from one edge of the 2½-inch-wide wire-edge sheer ribbon (floral on white). Pull the wire on the other edge of the ribbon to create 1 yard (.9 m) of tightly gathered ribbon. Bend both ends of the remaining wire to secure the gathered ribbon.

9. Fold over the cut edges of the gathered ribbon and hot glue them in place. Hot glue the gathered edge of the ribbon onto the bottom of the window shade, just above its wood slat.

10. To make the shade pull, fold in half the 8-inch (20.3 cm) piece of the 1½-inch-wide sheer ribbon (pink-and-white stripe). Hot glue the folded ribbon to the back side of the shade in the center of its bottom edge.

DESIGNER
ELIZABETH HELENE SEARLE

Folded Flower Pin

The clean look of sharp folds makes this ribbon flower thoroughly modern and stylish. Yielding an abundance of petals, this technique is one you'll definitely want to add to your repertoire. Whether created in white ribbon for the bride or in basic black for a cocktail dress, this simple yet versatile flower pin will be your favorite new accessory.

What You Do

Approximately 3 yards (2.7 m) sheer ribbon, 1½ inches (3.8 cm) wide*

6 x 6 inches (15.2 x 15.2 cm) buckram**

6 x 6 inches (15.2 x 15.2 cm) commercial felt

Hot glue gun and glue sticks

Hand-sewing needle and thread, optional

Button or bead

Pin backing

* Depending on how closely you space your points, more or less ribbon may be required.

** Buckram is a firm, coarse cotton fabric used for stiffening garments and in bookbinding.

1. If the ribbon has wire edges, remove the wires. Cut the ribbon into 3-inch (7.6 cm) lengths.

2. Cut the buckram to the desired pin shape. (This design is a paisley form.) Cut the felt to match the buckram.

3. Fold two corners of one edge of one 3-inch (7.6 cm) piece of ribbon to meet in the center of the opposite edge. Gather the lower edge of the folded ribbon, and secure with a needle and thread or thin craft wire. Repeat this process to make all the flower petals.

4. Starting at the lower edge, attach the flower petals to the buckram with the hot glue gun or a needle and thread. Overlap the petals as needed to cover raw edges.

5. Add a bead or a button to the center of the ribbon-covered pin. Hot glue the felt to the back of the buckram, and then glue the pin backing to the back of the felt. Let dry.

Open-Weave Pillows & Blankets

This project teaches you a simple method for introducing color into solid loose-weave fabrics. The results are both versatile and marvelous-looking. Here we feature a pair of pillows and a soft pastel baby blanket, but you can adapt this technique for other items, such as wearables, dish towels, and table linens.

WHAT YOU NEED

Loosely woven fabric, or item covered with loosely woven fabric

Mixed colors of grosgrain or satin ribbons, each long enough to run the width, height, or circumference of the fabric or item, in various widths

Needle, safety pin, or invisible tape

Hand-sewing needle and thread

What You Do

1. Determine where you'd like to weave the ribbons through the fabric. Clip and pull out the threads from the fabric at these points to create open areas in the fabric weave.

2. Affix a safety pin or needle to one end of one ribbon, or wrap the end with a piece of invisible tape to make it rigid. One at a time, weave the lengths of ribbon up and down through the open areas in the fabric weave.

3. Trim excess ribbon from the edges of the fabric. Hand-stitch the ends of the ribbon to secure.

Table Rays

For a sensational new look, spread a few ribbons across the top of your tablecloth before arranging the dinnerware. These stripes of brilliant color carry a lot of visual impact. Select the best ribbon to reflect the mood of your gathering. You can use grosgrain, satin, metallic, or sheer ribbon on top of anything from paper to vinyl to cloth.

WHAT YOU NEED

Tablecloth (can be fabric, vinyl, paper, or any other material)

Tape measure

Ribbon, colors and widths of your choice

Double-sided invisible tape, optional

What You Do

1. Measure the width of your tablecloth. Cut several lengths of ribbon to this measurement.

2. Place the cloth on the table. Arrange the ribbons on top of the cloth. If you wish to secure the ribbons in place, use small pieces of double-sided invisible tape.

The Eve of St. Andrews

Each year on November 29th and 30th, young Polish girls in search of a husband participate in many traditional fortune-telling games. In one, a scarf, a ribbon, and a rosary are hidden individually under three plates. The participant is blindfolded and turned around three times while the other girls rearrange the plates. The girl's eyes are uncovered and she must choose a plate. Her selection is uncovered and her future revealed: if she has selected a scarf she will be married; if it's a ribbon, she'll remain single another year; and if the rosary is her choice, she'll become a spinster or a nun.

Celestial Cloth

Ribbons play the starring role in this dynamic dining presentation. Their sprightly colors really grab your attention, especially when mounted on a translucent backing fabric.

Organza, organdy, or other sheer fabric, long enough to fit table

Approximately 8 yards (7.3 m) sheer woven-edge ribbon, 6 inches (15.2 cm) wide (blue), cut into six equal pieces

Approximately 4 yards (3.7 m) sheer woven-edge ribbon, 1½ inches (3.8 cm) wide (purple), cut into three equal pieces

Approximately 4 yards (3.7 m) sheer woven-edge ribbon, 1½ inches (3.8 cm) wide (green), cut into three equal pieces

Fusible webbing tape

Iron

Invisible thread

Sewing machine

What You Do

1. Lay the sheer fabric flat on top of a large worktable. Evenly space the sheer ribbons across the length of the fabric, placing one narrow ribbon between each wide ribbon. Alternate the colors of the narrow ribbons if you wish.

2. Following the manufacturer's instructions, use the iron to carefully fuse the sheer ribbon to the material.

3. Using the invisible thread, machine-stitch a hem around the edges of the cloth.

Handcrafted Cards

Blank greeting cards are a fantastic starting point for creating the right impression. These one-of-a-kind artworks adorned with ribbon, art papers, book text, and beads make a very sophisticated statement.

Elegant Collage Card

What You Do

1. Make the cut ends of the organza ribbon as straight as possible. Tape the two ends of the ribbon to the blank card. (This holds the ribbon in place while you sew.) Starting from the inside of the card, sew along the edges of the ribbon in a close running stitch. Continue sewing until all edges of the ribbons are stitched, removing the masking tape as you go. Always knot the thread on the inside of the card.

2. Coat the back of the 1-inch-wide (2.5 cm) dark ribbon with the glue, and carefully spread it down the center of the sheer ribbon. Use your fingertips to press down the ribbon surface, making sure all air bubbles release and the glue adheres well.

3. Using the ¾-inch-wide (1.9 cm) light ribbon, follow the procedure in step 2, centering the light ribbon on top of the dark ribbon. Let glue dry.

4. Thread the beading needle, and knot the thread. Starting from the bottom of the inside of the card, bring the needle up through the centerline of the light ribbon. Thread a single bead onto the needle, and pull it back through the original hole to the inside of the card. Bring the needle back up through the surface of the card approximately 1 inch (2.5 cm) away from the first hole. Add a bead, and go back through that hole. Continue this process until the last bead has been added at the top of the ribbon. Knot the thread inside the card, and cut off excess thread.

5. Cut the decorative paper to a desired width and length. Coat the back of the paper with glue, and adhere it to the top edge of the ribbon collage. (This covers rough edges while providing added visual interest.) Do the same for the bottom edge. Allow to dry.

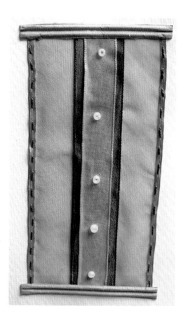

30 inches (76.2 cm) satin ribbon, ¾ inch (1.9 cm) wide, cut into 4-inch (10.2 cm) strips (dark green)

30 inches (76.2 cm) satin ribbon, ¾ inch (1.9 cm) wide, cut into 4-inch (10.2 cm) strips (light green)

3 x 5-inch (7.6 x 12.7 cm) piece of stiff paper

Masking tape

35 inches (88.9 cm) satin ribbon, ¾-inch (1.9 cm) wide, cut into 6-inch (15.2 cm) strips (white)

Clear-drying glue

5 x 7-inch (12.7 x 17.8 cm) blank greeting card

Craft knife

Seed beads, beading needle, and thread

Hot glue gun and glue sticks

Peek-A-Boo Weave Card

What You Do

1. Line up the green ribbons along the long edge of the 3 x 5-inch (7.6 x 12.7 cm) piece of stiff paper. Set the ribbons flush to each other, alternating colors as you go. Leave approximately ½ inch (1.3 cm) of ribbon hanging off the paper's edge.

2. Adhere a strip of masking tape to one end of the arranged ribbons. Wrap these ends around the back of the paper and tape them down. Use as much tape as you need to ensure the ribbons stay in place.

3. Line up the white ribbons along the narrow edge of the stiff paper. Set the ribbons flush to each other, leaving approximately ½ inch (1.3 cm) of ribbon hanging off the paper's edges.

4. Tape one end of the white ribbons to the stiff paper, as done in step 2, wrapping the taped edge around the paper and securing it to the back. (You should now have one secured edge and one loose edge for both the green and white ribbons.)

5. Work with one white ribbon at a time, weaving it under, and then over the green ribbons. When you reach the end of a white ribbon, tape it down to the back side of the stiff paper. Continue this process, alternating the weave, until all the ribbons are woven and secure.

6. Turn the stiff paper to the back side. Carefully remove one side of tape. Cover the ribbon ends with a thin layer of glue and press them down to the paper. Let dry. Continue removing the tape and gluing down the ribbon, one side at a time.

7. Place the piece of woven ribbon in the center of the inside of the card's cover and trace. Set the woven piece aside. Hold the front of the card up to the light to see the traced outline. This where the woven piece will show through the card.

8. Sketch a shape to be cut out of the front of the card. (In this design it's an oval, but you can use a circle, a square, or a more elaborate shape. Just be sure the cut out form fits inside the rectangular traced outline.) With the card open flat, cut out the sketched shape with a craft knife.

9. If you wish to add a beaded embellishment to the card cover, do so before attaching the section of woven ribbon. In this design, seed beads are sewn on to accent the rounded edge.

10. Dab a few dots of hot glue along the front edge of the piece of woven ribbon. Firmly press it onto the inside cover of the card, making sure the weave lines up inside your original traced outline.

Picture Window Card

What You Do

1. Make the cut ends of the organza ribbon as straight as possible. Tape two of the ribbon edges to the card. (This holds the ribbon in place while you sew.) Starting from the inside of the card, sew along the edge of the ribbon in a close running stitch. Stitch along three of the ribbon edges, removing the masking tape as you go. Leave the thread in the needle.

2. Slide the paper scrap through the opening and place it underneath the ribbon. Trim the paper as needed. Slip the found objects through the opening. They should lie under the ribbon but on top of the paper. Don't glue these objects down—they should be free to move under the sheer ribbon.

3. Sew a running stitch along the last edge to close the ribbon "window." Knot the thread on the inside of the card to secure.

4½-inch (11.4 cm) piece organza ribbon, 3 inches (7.6 cm) wide

Masking tape

5 x 7-inch (12.7 x 17.8 cm) blank greeting card

Hand-sewing needle and thread

Paper scrap (handwritten letter, page from an old book, etc.)

Found objects (beads, metal charms, pressed or silk leaves or flowers, etc.)

DESIGNER
MARVIS A. LUTZ

Heart-to-Heart Sachet

Welcome soothing scents into your home with this charming heart sachet. Fill it with dried herbs, aromatic potpourri, perfumed stuffing, or anything your heart desires. These sachets are so quick and easy to create, you can sew several in a flash. They're great as last-minute gifts or to top off a wrapped package.

WHAT YOU NEED

Ribbon for sachet, length three times its width, such as 9 x 3 inches (22.9 x 7.6 cm)

Sewing machine

Sachet filling, such as lavender, polyester stuffing, etc.

Hand-sewing needle and thread

½ yard (45.7 cm) bias-cut silk ribbon, more than 1 inch (2.5 cm) wide

½ yard (45.7 cm) silk or satin ribbon, ¼ inch (6 mm) wide

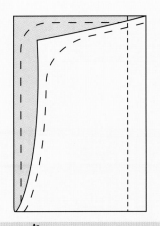

Figure 1

What You Do

1. Fold the sachet ribbon in half with its right sides together. Using a ¼-inch (6 mm) seam allowance, machine-stitch down one long edge of the ribbon.

2. Use a double thread and a loose running stitch to sew the rest of the ribbon, as shown in figure 1. Turn the ribbon right side out, and then gently pull up the gathering thread. Push up the corners of the heart.

3. Fill the ribbon sachet with lavender, polyester stuffing, or whatever you wish. Pull the gathers tight, and then stitch the sachet closed.

4. Cut small lengths of the ¼-inch-wide (6 mm) silk or satin ribbon, tie a decorative knot in one end of each piece, and attach them to the top of the sachet. Cover the small ribbon lengths with a simple ribbon flower (see pages 19 and 20 for ideas).

Jumping the Broom

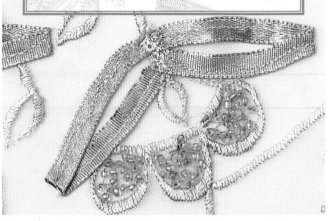

Marriages between African-Americans were prohibited during slavery, so many rituals were created to celebrate a couple's union. Jumping the broom became a symbolic act of sweeping away one's old life and welcoming a new beginning. Often before the ceremony, the bride and bridesmaids decorated the broom with ribbons and bows. To nurture community involvement in the marriage, a basket of ribbons may have been present at the wedding. Family and friends tied ribbon pieces onto the broom in a symbolic offer of support.

DESIGNER
SALLY BRYENTON

Snapshot Scrapbook

Natural colors and textures give this handcrafted photo album a warm, handsome appearance. Sturdy ribbons become decorative hinges that bind the covers to the book's spine. Why not embellish the album's jacket with mementos of a vacation or special occasion?

What You Do

2 matte boards, each 10 x 12 inches (25.4 x 30.5 cm)

Craft knife

¼ yard (22.9 cm) fabric of your choice (brown suede)

5 x 4-inch (12.7 x 10.2 cm) photo album*

¾ yard (68.6 cm) jacquard or other patterned ribbon, ½ inch (1.3 cm) wide (brown and black motif)

Fabric glue

Fusible webbing tape, ½ inch (1.3 cm) wide

1 yard (.9 m) satin ribbon, 1 inch (2.5 cm) wide (black)

¼ yard (22.9 cm) grosgrain ribbon, ⅝ inch (1.6 cm) wide (white)

6 inches (15.2 cm) grosgrain ribbon, ⅝ inch (1.6 cm) wide (brown)

Thin decorative cording or trim

6 assorted beads or buttons

*Our album has exposed binding hinges. These slide out so the ribbon loops can be attached.

1. Use a craft knife to cut three pieces of matte board, each 5 x 4¼ inches (12.7 x 10.8 cm). Cut a fourth piece of matte board that is 5 x 4 inches (12.7 x 10.2 cm).

2. Cut three pieces of fabric, each 5 x 4¼ inches (12.7 x 10.8 cm). Cut a fourth piece of fabric, 5 x 4 inches (12.7 x 10.2 cm).

3. Remove the album's hinges. Cut seven pieces of the ½-inch-wide (1.3 cm) jacquard or other patterned ribbon (brown and black motif), each 2 inches (5 cm) long. Feed two pieces of the cut ribbon side by side through the front of the album spine, 1 inch (2.5 cm) down from the top edge. Feed two more pieces of ribbon, side by side and 1 inch (2.5 cm) up from the bottom edge. Halve the length of each ribbon, and glue each end to one side of one of the larger matte board pieces.

4. Feed the remaining 2-inch-long (5 cm) ribbon hinge pieces through the back spine of the album. Position one ribbon hinge in the center, and one each at the top and the bottom of the back spine. Halve the length of each ribbon, and glue each end to one side of one of the larger matte board pieces.

5. Use the fabric glue to adhere the fabric pieces to both sides of the appropriately-sized pieces of matte board. Let dry.

6. Following the manufacturer's instructions, use the webbing tape to fuse pieces of the 1-inch-wide (2.5 cm) satin ribbon (black) around each edge of the fabric-covered matte boards.

7. Embellish the front of the album with the grosgrain ribbons, thin decorative cording, and beads as desired.

8. Cut a length of the ⅝-inch-wide (1.6 cm) grosgrain ribbon (white) and of the ½-inch-wide (1.3 cm) jacquard or other patterned ribbon (brown and black motif). Turn under and hem the ends of these ribbons to fit the length of the book. Adhere the ribbon lengths to the underside of the long edge of the album cover.

9. Glue the smaller piece of matte board on top of the album's front cover, sandwiching the ribbon hinges. Let dry. Glue the last piece of matte board on the back of the album's back cover, sandwiching the ribbon hinges. Let dry.

DESIGNER
JOAN K. MORRIS

Tapestry Pillow

Do you rummage through the remnant bins, buy scraps of fabric with irresistible designs, and then wait for the perfect project? This pillow pattern displays upholstery remnants in a most clever way. The diverse fabrics come together under a ruffled satin ribbon. The technique is easy and the results are glorious.

5 upholstery fabric remnants (see cut list below)*

Sewing machine

Iron

3½ yards (3.2 m) satin ribbon, 1½ inches (3.8 cm) wide

Hand-sewing needle and thread

16 x 16-inch (40.6 x 40.6 cm) pillow form

*The fabric measurements for this pillow are: 17 x 17 inches (43.2 x 43.2 cm) for the pillow back; 8 x 8 inches (20.3 x 20.3 cm) for the center square; 6 x 17 inches (15.2 x 43.2 cm) for each side panel; and 6 x 8 inches (15.2 x 20.3 cm) for the top and the bottom panels. Select and cut your remnants according to these dimensions.

What You Do

1. Using a ½-inch (1.3 cm) seam allowance, machine-stitch the center fabric square to the top and bottom panels. (Always make sure the fabric designs are correctly oriented on the pillow.) Iron the seams toward the center.

2. Using a ½-inch (1.3 cm) seam allowance, machine-stitch each side panel to the center panel extended in step 1. Iron the seams toward the center.

3. Measure the perimeter of the center square of fabric, and cut a piece of the satin ribbon that is twice this measurement. Following figure 1a, use invisible or matching thread to machine- or hand-baste the cut ribbon in a zigzag pattern.

4. Pull the top basting thread to gather the ribbon so it fits around the pillow's center square (figure 1b). Stitch the gathered ribbon to the center square by machine or by hand.

5. Measure from each corner of the center fabric square down the seam line to the edge of the pillow cover. Cut four pieces of ribbon to this length. Place the four lengths of ribbon on top of the exposed pillow-cover seams. If possible, hide one end of each ribbon under the gathered ribbon. Machine- or hand-stitch both edges of the ribbon to the fabric cover.

6. Position the pieced pillow front and the back fabric panel right sides together, and pin. Using a ½-inch (1.3 cm) seam allowance, stitch the around the pillow. Leave an 8-inch (20.3 cm) opening in the cover.

7. Turn the stitched fabric right side out, and push out the corners. Stuff the pillow form into the pillow cover, and hand-stitch closed.

Variation: This ribbon treatment can be hand-sewn onto a store-bought pillow.

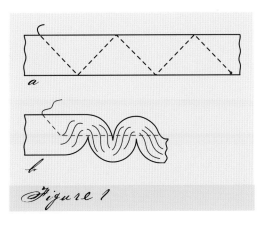

Figure 1

DESIGNER
JOAN K. MORRIS

Pleased-to-Meet-You Mat

Offer the warmest of welcomes by placing this cheerful grass mat at the foot of any doorway. Lengths of grosgrain ribbons in vibrant shades weave through the mat and tie off in back, forming a simple floral design. Jazz up the edges of the mat with ribbon fringe.

WHAT YOU NEED

6 yards (5.5 m) grosgrain ribbon, ³⁄₈ inch (9.5 mm) wide (green)

3 yards (2.7 m) grosgrain ribbon, ³⁄₈ inch (9.5 mm) wide (purple)

18 x 30-inch (45.7 x 76.2 cm) woven grass doormat

2 yards (1.8 m) jacquard ribbon, 1 inch (2.5 cm) wide

4 yards (3.7 m) grosgrain ribbon, 1 inch (2.5 cm) wide (purple)

4 yards (3.7 m) grosgrain ribbon, ⁵⁄₈ inch (1.6 cm) wide (yellow)

½ yard (45.7 cm) grosgrain ribbon, 1 inch (2.5 cm) wide (red)

Fabric glue or hot glue gun and glue sticks

Important: Grass doormats are very uneven, so all measurements given for this projects are approximate. Experiment with weaving the ribbon through the mat before cutting the ribbon to size.

What You Do

1. Measure and cut the ³⁄₈-inch (9.5 mm) grosgrain ribbon (green) into 12 pieces, each 11 inches (27.9 cm) long. Measure and cut the ³⁄₈-inch (9.5 mm) grosgrain ribbon (purple) into six pieces, each 11 inches (27.9 cm) long.

2. Tie nine pieces of the ribbon cut in step 1 onto each 18-inch (45.7 cm) edge of the doormat, alternating the colors. (Our design follows this sequence: green, purple, green, green, purple, green, green, purple, green.)

3. From the bottom left corner of the mat, measure approximately 5 inches (12.7 cm) over and 5 inches (12.7 cm) up from the edge. Insert the jacquard ribbon at this point. Weave in and out of the mat, maintaining the 5-inch (12.5 cm) border, to create a rectangle. When the ribbon ends meet, tie them in a knot underneath the mat.

4. Starting at the bottom left corner of the mat, weave the 1-inch-wide (2.5 cm) grosgrain ribbon (purple) up to the corner of the jacquard ribbon rectangle, and then back down to the edge of the mat. Repeat this angled weave all the way across the length of the mat to the bot-

tom right corner. (This makes one side of a ribbon X.)

5. Measure 5 inches (12.7 cm) up from the bottom left corner of the mat, and insert the ⁵⁄₈-inch-wide (1.6 cm) grosgrain ribbon (yellow). Under the mat, tie the end of the ribbon to the ribbon woven in step 4. Weave the ⁵⁄₈-inch-wide (1.6 cm) grosgrain ribbon (yellow) down to the edge of the mat, and then up to the edge of the jacquard ribbon rectangle. This ribbon can be woven over or under the first angled weave (step 4) to complete the ribbon X. Repeat this angled weave all the way across the length of the mat.

6. Repeat steps 4 and 5 on the top 30-inch (76.2 cm) edge of the doormat.

7. At the center of the jacquard ribbon rectangle's lower border, insert the ³⁄₈-inch-wide (9.5 mm) grosgrain ribbon (green) and tie a knot underneath the mat. To make the flower stem, insert the other end of the ribbon 3 inches (7.6 cm) up and pull to tighten. Under the mat, reinsert the loose ribbon end at the bottom of the stem, and, approximately 2½ inches (6.4 cm) away, weave it back under the mat to form a leaf. Make a second leaf on

the opposite side of the stem.

8. Repeat step 7 to create two more stems with leaves on either side of the first. Center the stems within the jacquard ribbon rectangle.

9. To make a flower, start by weaving a ³⁄₈-inch-wide (9.5 mm) grosgrain ribbon (yellow) at the top of the center stem. Weave up 2½ inches (6.4 cm), and then back down to the stem. Weave one 2-inch (5 cm) petal on each side of center petal. Knot the ribbon under the mat to secure.

10. To create the petals above each remaining stem, weave the ³⁄₈-inch-wide (9.5 mm) grosgrain ribbon (purple) six times around in 2-inch (5 cm) lengths. Tie off each ribbon under the mat.

11. Measure and cut two 8-inch (20.3 cm) pieces of the 1-inch-wide (2.5 cm) grosgrain ribbon (red). Weave one of these ribbon pieces around the center of each purple flower and tie it off under the mat.

12. Trim off excess ribbon from the knots under the mat. Dab each knot with fabric glue or hot glue to secure.

Glamour Shade

Rings of ruffled ribbons give this ordinary lamp shade a makeover in true Hollywood style. Emitting a soft glow of tinted light, this lamp adapts to any room with a simple change of ribbon colors or patterns. Roll out the red carpet, and get ready for your close-up.

What You Do

Lamp and lamp shade

Tape measure

2 yards (1.8 m) each of three shades of metallic sheer wire-edged ribbon, 2½ inches (6.4 cm) wide (olive, gold, and plum metallic)*

Hand-sewing needle

Invisible thread

2 yards (1.8 m) metallic, sheer, and textured wire edge ribbon, 2½ inches (6.4 cm) wide, in coordinating shades*

*The amount of ribbon required may increase or decrease depending upon your lamp shade. These ribbon lengths are based upon a curved lamp shade that is 6 inches (15.2 cm) tall, has a 32-inch (81.3 cm) circumference at the bottom opening, and a 13-inch (33 cm) circumference at the top.

1. Starting at the top of the lamp shade, measure its circumference at 1-inch (2.5 cm) intervals, and record these dimensions. Assign alternating colors of the metallic sheer wired ribbons for each of the measurements. Cut the ribbons 2 inches (5 cm) longer than the circumference measurement.

2. Using the invisible thread, hand-stitch the cut ends of each ribbon together to form loops. Slide the loops over the outside of the lamp shade, alternating ribbon colors.

3. Using the invisible thread and hand-sewing needle, tack down each ribbon loop. Bend the wires of the tacked ribbon loops to create ruffles or any other desired effect.

4. To create a scalloped ribbon edge on the bottom of the lamp shade, cut a piece of the textured ribbon two and one-half times the circumference of the bottom of the shade. Using the invisible thread and hand-sewing needle, make a running stitch through the center of the ribbon. Pull the thread to gather the ribbon. Tack this piece to the bottom edge of the shade.

Trace of Taffeta Wreath

Colored ribbon brings a touch of elegance to any ordinary dried flower wreath. As this design illustrates, ribbons contribute hues and textures that flatter dried materials to create a warmer welcome.

**10 yards (9.1 m)
wire-edge
taffeta ribbon,
approximately
2 inches (5 cm) wide**

Floral picks

Craft wire

Dried flower wreath

2 floral pins

What You Do

1. Cut the wire-edge taffeta ribbon into 8-inch (20.3 cm) lengths. Start with 20 or 30 lengths, cutting more later as needed.

2. Fold one 8-inch (20.3 cm) length of ribbon in half. Wrap the cut ends around a floral pick and secure them with craft wire. Using this method, wire two or three more lengths of ribbon to the same floral pick.

3. Insert the ribbon-decorated floral pick into the dried flower wreath.

4. Repeat steps 2 and 3 as often as desired until you've covered the wreath to your liking.

5. To create the ribbon hanger, cut a piece of wire-edge taffeta long enough to suit your needs. (This design uses an 18-inch [45.7 cm] piece of ribbon.) Fold the ribbon in half, and use the floral pins to attach it to the back of the wreath.

DESIGNER
ELIZABETH HELENE SEARLE

Summer Sun Hat

Plant a ribbon-flower garden atop a plain straw hat, and you'll have everlasting blooms everyone admires. Perfect for picnics, garden parties, or just lounging by the pool, this colorful sun shield is sure to become a perennial favorite.

WHAT YOU NEED

Straw hat

Ribbon or netting to fit around the hat's circumference

Straight pins

Hot glue gun and glue stick or hand-sewing needle and thread

Assorted ribbon flowers, see pages 19 and 20 for basic instructions

What You Do

1. Make a band around the hat with the ribbon or netting. Hot glue the band to secure. (If desired, you can use several hand stitches instead of hot glue to secure the decorations to the hat.)

2. Arrange assorted ribbon flowers and leaves on the hat until you're pleased with the design. Pin the ribbon flowers and leaves in place, and then individually hot glue or stitch them to secure.

DESIGNER
JOAN K. MORRIS

Perfect Vision Valet

Forever hunting for your spectacles? Your eyeglasses will never go missing if they're safely tucked inside this soft handcrafted bag that hangs around your neck, and you'll look incredibly stylish, too! This project shows that adding one piece of spectacular ribbon enhances any design.

What You Do

- ⅛ **yard (11.4 cm) satin fabric**

- ½ **yard (45.7 cm) fusible interfacing**

- **Iron and ironing board**

- **Straight pins**

- ½ **yard (45.7 cm) jacquard ribbon, 3 inches (7.6 cm) wide**

- **Sewing machine**

- **Invisible thread**

- **Hand-sewing needle**

- **6 gold rings**

- **2 yards (1.8 m) cording**

- **2 glass beads with large holes for cording**

1. Measure and cut two 5 x 15-inch (12.7 x 38.1 cm) pieces of the satin fabric. Measure and cut one 4¾ x 14¾-inch (12.1 x 37.5 cm) piece of fusible interfacing. Following the manufacturer's instructions, center and then iron the fusible interfacing onto the wrong side of one of the satin pieces.

2. Pin the jacquard ribbon in the center and down the length of the right side of the interfaced satin fabric. Machine-stitch each edge, leaving ½ inch (1.3 cm) of ribbon unsewn near the top and bottom cut ends.

3. Fold the ribbon-embellished satin fabric in half lengthwise with its right sides together. Pin in place. Using a ½-inch (1.3 cm) seam allowance, machine-stitch down both sides of the fabric. Turn the sewn fabric right side out.

4. Fold the plain piece of satin fabric in half lengthwise with its right sides together. Pin in place. Using a ½-inch (1.3 cm) seam allowance, machine-stitch down both sides of the fabric, but don't turn it right side out. Fold the open edges of the fabric over ½ inch (1.3 cm), and iron in place. (This is the lining for the eyeglass case.)

5. Place the lining inside the case, and line up all side seams. Fold over the top edge of the ribbon to match the top of the lining. Leaving the ribbon out, hand-stitch all the way around the top edge to join the satin fabrics.

6. Turn under and machine-stitch a ½-inch (1.3 cm) hem on the ribbon's cut end. Fold the remaining ribbon over the case's edge and hand-stitch it inside.

7. On the back side of the eyeglass case, evenly position three gold rings on one edge of the ribbon. Hand-sew to secure. Repeat this process on the other edge of the ribbon.

8. From the top of the eyeglass case, run one end of the cord through three rings on one ribbon edge. Run the other end of the cord through the rings on the opposite ribbon edge. String one glass bead on each end of the cord. Adjust the cord's length as desired, and then tie a tight knot under each bead to secure.

DESIGNER
JOAN K. MORRIS

Keepsake Gift Bag

To make an elegant, memorable presentation, tuck a bottle of wine or flavored oil inside this spectacular bag. This exquisite gift wrapping is made entirely of ribbons, utilizing a technique that is both quick and easy.

2 yards (1.8 m) scalloped-edge metallic ribbon, 4 inches (10.2 cm) wide

1 yard (.9 m) velvet ribbon, 2½ inches (6.4 cm) wide

Sewing machine

Invisible thread

Wine or other bottle

Straight pins

Fabric glue or fray retardant (optional)

24-inch (61 cm) metallic cord with tassel ends

What You Do

1. Cut the metallic ribbon in half. Place the velvet ribbon face up in the center of one length of the metallic ribbon. Machine-stitch both edges of the velvet ribbon to the metallic ribbon. Turn the stitched piece face down on your worktable.

2. Position the second piece of metallic ribbon perpendicular to the first piece. (The ribbons intersect to form a cross.) Machine-stitch the intersection of the ribbons, making a square, and then stitch across the square, making an X. (This is the bottom of the wine bag.)

3. Place the wine or other bottle on top of the X sewn at the bottom of the bag. Pull up all four ribbon ends to the top of the bottle. Pin the ribbons to hold them in place.

4. With the scalloped edges of the metallic ribbons facing out, pin the adjoining ribbon edges together. Pin all four ribbon edges evenly but not too tightly. Remove the wine bottle from the bag. Machine-stitch all four pinned edges of the bag.

5. Turn the top edges of the ribbons toward the inside of the bag to form a double-folded hem. Machine- or hand-stitch the hem in place.

6. Measure and make a mark approximately 5 inches (12.7 cm) down from the top of the bag on all four scalloped ribbon edges. Create a vertical buttonhole just inside the sewn edges at these points, or simply make a small slice in the ribbon and stabilize it with fabric glue or fray retardant. Run the tasseled cord through the buttonholes, and tie a bow.

DESIGNER
SALLY BRYENTON

Silky Lingerie Bag

When packing your suitcase, use this silky bag to protect your lingerie. Select supple fabrics so your delicate items smoothly slip inside. Creating a ribbon design of assorted colors and textures is a wonderful way to express your softer side.

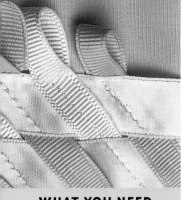

2 yards (1.8 m) satin ribbon, ½ inch (1.3 cm) wide (lavender)

1 yard (.9 m) satin ribbon, ½ inch (1.3 cm) wide (light green)

1¼ yards (1.1 m) satin ribbon, ½ inch (1.3 cm) wide (white)

10 x 20-inch (25.4 x 50.8 cm) piece of fabric for top of bag (light blue)

Hand-sewing needle

Invisible thread

1½ yards (1.4 m) grosgrain ribbon, ⅜ inch (9.5 mm) wide (white)

2 yards (1.8 m) grosgrain ribbon, ⅜ inch (9.5 mm) wide (aqua)

Sewing machine

Iron

6 x 20-inch (15.2 x 50.8 cm) piece of fabric for bottom of bag (lavender)

1 yard (.9 m) grosgrain ribbon, ¼ inch (6 mm) wide (light blue)

What You Do

1. Cut one 20-inch (50.8 cm) piece of each of the three ½-inch-wide (1.3 cm) satin ribbons. Lay the cut ribbon pieces horizontally in the center of the 10 x 20-inch (25.4 x 50.8 cm) fabric piece (light blue). Tack the ends of the ribbon to hold them in place.

2. Cut five 4-inch (10.2 cm) pieces of each of the two colors of ⅜-inch-wide (9.5 mm) grosgrain ribbon.

3. Alternating colors, weave five of the cut grosgrain ribbons over and under the satin ribbons placed in step 1. Angle the weave away from what will be the center of the bag. Tack the short ribbons in place, folding the top end of each grosgrain ribbon under the top satin ribbon to make a decorative loop.

4. Repeat step 3 to weave the remaining five short ribbons. This time, fold the bottom end of each grosgrain ribbon under the bottom satin ribbon to make the loop. Machine-stitch all tacked ribbons to secure.

5. Fold over the top edge of the top bag fabric ¾ inch (1.9 cm), and press with an iron. Cut a 20-inch (50.8 cm) piece of the ½-inch-wide (1.3 cm) satin ribbon (lavender). Place the ribbon ⅛-inch (3 mm) down from the top edge of the bag, and carefully machine-stitch, sewing close to the ribbon edges.

6. Create four buttonholes in the center of the ribbon sewn in step 5: one in the middle of the front; one in the middle of the rear; and one on each side.

7. Cut 12 pieces of the ½-inch-wide (1.3 cm) satin ribbon, each 6 inches (15.2 cm) long (10 white and two lavender). Cut four pieces of ribbon 20 inches (50.8 cm) long (two aqua grosgrain, one white grosgrain, and one light green satin).

8. Lay out the fabric for the bottom of the bag (lavender). Space the 6-inch (15.2 cm) ribbon pieces cut in step 7 at ½-inch (1.3 cm) intervals along the top edge of the fabric. Tack the top end of each ribbon. Use a simple over-and-under technique to weave the 20-inch (50.8 cm) ribbon pieces through the 6-inch (15.2 cm) ribbon pieces. Tack the intersections of the ribbons to secure.

9. Using a ¼-inch (6 mm) seam allowance, machine-stitch the top bag fabric to the bottom bag fabric. Press the seam with an iron. Cut, and then machine-stitch a 20-inch (50.8 cm) piece of ½-inch-wide (1.3 cm) satin ribbon (lavender) on top of the seam, all the way around the bag.

10. With the wrong sides together, stitch the back bag seam with a ½-inch (1.3 cm) seam allowance. Trim the seam to ⅜ inch (9.5 mm), turn the fabric inside out, and press. With the right sides together, stitch the back bag seam with a ½-inch (1.3 cm) seam allowance. This technique results in a neat double-folded hem.

11. Feed one end of the ¼-inch-wide (6 mm) grosgrain ribbon (light blue) in and out of the buttonholes. Tie the ribbon into a bow to close.

DESIGNER
KATE KOHN

Picture Perfect Wall Hanging

Color photocopying is a wonderful tool for creating image-based crafts without altering original photographs. To make this wall hanging, a graduation portrait was enlarged, quartered, mounted on boards, and embellished with ribbons. You can choose different materials to fit a certain theme, such as a new baby or a favorite pet.

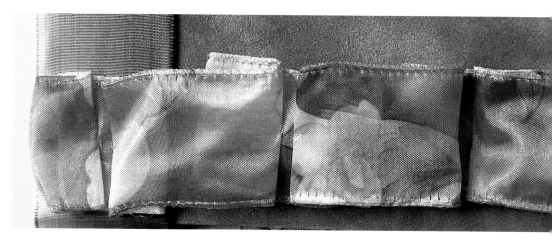

2 wood dowels, each 19 inches (48.3 cm) long, ⅜ inch (9.5 mm) in diameter

4 wood craft tips to fit ends of dowels, ½ inch (1.3 cm) in diameter

Wood stain and brush

8 x 7-inch (20.3 x 17.8 cm) color photocopied snapshot

4 pieces light-colored matte board, each 5¼ x 5¼ inches (13.3 x 13.3 cm)

32 photo corners

Clear-drying craft glue

4 pieces dark-colored matte board, each 10 x 8 inches (25.4 x 20.3 cm)

21 x 17-inch (53.3 x 43.2 cm) piece of backing fabric (will show)

Iron

Hot glue gun and glue stick

2½ yards (2.3 m) ombré ribbon, 1½ inches (3.8 cm) wide (green)

1 yard (.9 m) nonwired ombré ribbon, 1 inch (2.5 cm) wide (brown)

2½ yards (2.3 m) wired sheer ribbon, 1½ inches (3.8 cm) wide (floral)

Hand-sewing needle

Invisible thread

What You Do

1. Stain the wood dowels and craft tips, following the manufacturer's instructions. Set aside to dry.

2. Cut the color photocopied snapshot into equal quarters, each 4 x 3½ inches (10.2 x 8.9 cm).

3. Glue one photo corner to each corner of all four pieces of light-colored matte board. Let dry.

4. Position the top edge of one of the light-colored matte boards 2 inches (5 cm) below the top edge of one of the dark-colored matte boards. Center the light board between the left and right edges of the dark board. Glue the matte board in this position. Repeat this process for all remaining pairs.

5. Slip four photo corners onto each snapshot quarter. Adhere the corners in the center of the light-colored matte board.

6. If needed, press the backing fabric with an iron, and then lay the fabric right side up on your work surface. Arrange the four matted images into a rectangular grid on top of the fabric. Leave a 1-inch (2.5 cm) border of exposed fabric between each board. Lightly mark the fabric to indicate the positions of the boards.

7. Use the hot glue gun to adhere the four matted images in a level and evenly spaced grid.

8. Cut two pieces of the 1½-inch-wide (3.8 cm) unwired ombré ribbon to fit the side edges of the project. With fabric glue, adhere the ribbons to the outer edges of the matte boards and the fabric; then fold the ribbon's outer edge around to the back of the project.

9. Cut eight 4-inch (10.2 cm) lengths of the 1-inch-wide (2.5 cm) unwired ombré ribbon (brown). Fold these pieces in half to make 2-inch (5 cm) loops.

10. Starting 1 inch (2.5 cm) in from one side edge, evenly space four loops across the top edge of the project. Hot glue the ends of the ribbon loops to the back of the project. Repeat this step on the bottom edge of the project.

11. Measure the width of the project at its center. Double this number, and cut a piece of the 1½-inch-wide (3.8 cm) wired sheer ribbon (floral) to match the doubled dimension. Create box pleats along the ribbon's length, as shown in figure 1,

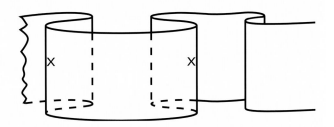

Figure 1

tacking the outer edges of each pleat in the center of the ribbon. Hot glue the ribbon in place.

12. Create a second small piece of box-pleated 1½-inch-wide (3.8 cm) wired sheer ribbon to fit between the lower matte boards. Hot glue to secure.

13. Create a third small piece of box-pleated 1½-inch-wide (3.8 cm) wired sheer ribbon to fit at the top of the project, centered between the border ribbon, fabric, and matte boards. Hot glue to secure.

14. Run the dowels through the ribbon loops, one at the top and one at the bottom of the wall hanging. Use hot glue to attach one craft tip to each dowel end.

DESIGNER
BARBARA ZARETSKY

Lovely Linen Place Mat & Napkin

Use this casual combination of linen fabric and grosgrain ribbon to set a tasteful table. It's the simple sophistication of stripes that gives this pair its classic style. The natural easy-going hues of flax and olive complement a fresh summer feast, but you can modify the colors for any occasion.

2 pieces linen fabric, each 15½ x 20 inches (39.4 x 50.8 cm)

6 pieces grosgrain ribbon, each 15½ inches (39.4 cm) long, 1 inch (2.5 cm) wide

Straight pins

Hand-sewing needle and thread

Iron

What You Do

PLACE MAT

Finished dimensions: 14½ x 19 inches (36.8 x 48.3 cm)

1. Pin all six ribbons, evenly spaced, onto one of the fabric pieces. Staying as close to the edges as possible, sew down each side of each ribbon.

2. Lay the fabric on your work surface with the ribbons facing up. Pin the second, unembellished, piece of fabric on top.

3. Using a ½-inch (1.3 cm) seam allowance, sew around three sides of the mat. Sew three-quarters of the fourth side closed. Turn the sewn fabric right side out through the opening, making sure the corners are flat.

4. Use an iron to press the seams. Turn under the opening ½ inch (1.3 cm) to match the seam allowance. Use a hand-sewing needle and thread to slip-stitch the opening closed, as shown in figure 1. Press the mat flat.

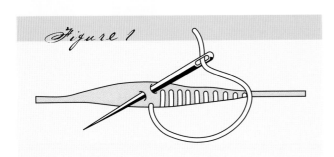

Figure 1

**22 x 22-inch
(55.9 x 55.9 cm) piece
of linen fabric**

Iron

**Hand-sewing needle
and thread**

Straight pins

Sewing machine

**2 grosgrain ribbons,
each 21 inches
(53.3 cm) long, 1 inch
(2.5 cm) wide**

What You Do

NAPKIN

Finished dimensions: 20 x 20 inches (50.8 x 50.8 cm)

1. Turn in all raw edges of the linen fabric to make a ½-inch (1.3 cm) double hem. Use the iron to press the fold lines.

2. Open out the folds, and cut off a triangle of fabric diagonally across each corner, as shown in figure 2a. Fold a single hem diagonally across the corners, as shown in figure 2b. Iron the folds, and then baste them down either by hand or machine.

3. Taking each corner in turn, fold in the first fold of the hem on one side of the fabric. Turn in the first fold on the adjacent side, and then make the second fold of the hem on both sides. Pin the folds in place (see figure 2c).

4. Machine-stitch around the fabric, staying close to the inner folded edge and pivoting at the corners. Remove the basting stitches and iron the fabric.

5. Fold under and press a ½-inch (1.3 cm) hem on each cut end of the two 21-inch (53.3 cm) ribbon pieces.

6. Position the ribbon ½ inch (1.3 cm) in from one finished napkin edge, lining up the pressed ribbon ends with the napkin hems. Pin the ribbons in place. Repeat this on the opposite edge of the napkin. Staying as close to the edges as possible, sew down each side of each ribbon. Press the napkin with an iron.

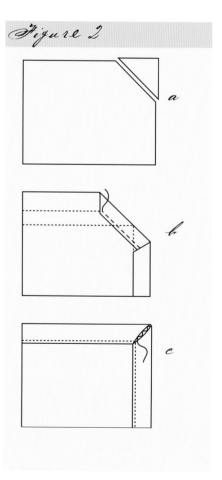

Figure 2

DESIGNER

ELIZABETH HELENE SEARLE

Pin Pillow

Why tuck your jewelry into a dark drawer when you can show it off atop this charming display? The sewing pattern is so simple, you'll have no trouble creating the base. To give the pillow an antique look, first add a piece of lace or a fabric doily, and then your choice of ribbon flowers.

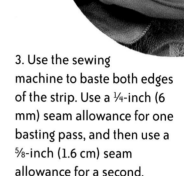

WHAT YOU NEED

½ **yard (45.7 cm) fabric**

Hand-sewing needle and thread

Sewing machine

Polyester stuffing

Ribbon flower and leaves (see pages 19–20 for basic instructions)

What You Do

1. Cut two fabric circles, each 7 inches (17.8 cm) in diameter. Cut one fabric strip, 3½ inches (8.9 cm) by the width of the fabric, approximately 45 inches (114.3 cm).

2. Place the two short ends of the fabric strip together with the right sides facing each other. Using a regular hand stitch and a ¼-inch (6 mm) seam allowance, sew the ends together for approximately ½ inch (1.3 cm). Switch to a longer basting stitch, and sew the ends together for approximately 2 inches (5 cm). Use a regular hand stitch to sew the remaining ½ inch (1.3 cm) of fabric together. (This stitching sequence is illustrated in figure 1. The basting stitches will later be opened for stuffing.) Press open the seam.

3. Use the sewing machine to baste both edges of the strip. Use a ¼-inch (6 mm) seam allowance for one basting pass, and then use a ⅝-inch (1.6 cm) seam allowance for a second.

4. Divide one fabric circle into quarters, as shown in figure 2, marking each point with a straight pin. (This helps to evenly distribute the gathers.)

5. Divide the strip into quarters. With their right sides together, gather the strip, distribute the gathers evenly around the circle, and pin in place. Stitch the strip to the circle using a ½-inch (1.3 cm) seam allowance. Repeat this process with the second fabric circle on the other side of the strip.

6. Open the basting stitches made in step 2. Turn the cushion right side out, stuff it firmly, and then stitch the opening closed.

7. If desired, hand-stitch a piece of lace or a fabric doily to the top of the cushion. Add any ribbon flower that appeals to you. You may wish to use the ribbon rose on page 19 or the pointed petal flower on page 20.

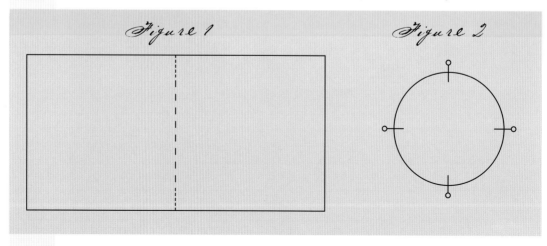

Figure 1

Figure 2

The Sneud

Long ago on the Orkney Islands, every young girl wore a ribbon in her hair called a *sneud.* A symbol of virginity, the sneud was removed by the mother of the bride when the young girl was dressed for her wedding. Once the festivities were over, the mother of the bride and her close friends placed the girl's sneud on a hot stone taken from the fire. The women elders predicted the bride's future, chiefly her fertility and wealth, by observing the ribbon's shape as it burned.

Periwinkle Passion Wreath

Combine shimmering satin ribbon roses with vibrant layers of netting to create this front-door dazzler. Use any color scheme you wish to reflect the spirit of the season, complement your home's decor, or enhance a party theme.

WHAT YOU NEED

3½ yards (3.2 m) satin ribbon, 5 to 6 inches (12.7 to 15.2 cm) wide

Floral picks

Craft wire

Polystyrene wreath base

3 pieces of netting fabric, 1 yard (.9 m) each, in three different colors

What You Do

1. Cut 10 pieces of the satin ribbon, each 12 inches (30.5 cm) long.

2. To make a rose, fold one satin ribbon in half lengthwise. Loosely roll the folded ribbon. Wire the rolled ribbon onto a floral pick. Fluff out the ribbon rose to adjust its "petals."

3. Repeat step 2 to make a total of 10 roses. Insert the roses artistically around the wreath base.

4. Cut all three pieces of netting fabric into 6 x 6-inch (15.2 x 15.2 cm) squares. Divide the squares into three single-color piles.

5. Make a layered set of three netting squares, putting the darkest color on the bottom and the lightest on the top. Bunch up the layered squares in the center, and then wire the center to a floral pick. Insert the pick into the wreath base.

6. Repeat step 5 to make enough bunched netting squares to cover the wreath base.

Travel Pouch

When you need to carry just a few items and want to keep your hands free, this small nylon pouch is a practical solution. The carabiner, a hiking gadget, hooks the travel pouch to your belt loop, giving you an extra pocket. Ribbons are fed through the woven nylon webbing for a decorative flourish.

98

6 x 6-inch (15.2 x 15.2 cm) piece of sturdy fabric, such as nylon or canvas

Sewing machine

1 yard (.9 m) nylon webbing, 1 inch (2.5 cm) wide (navy)

1 yard (.9 m) nylon webbing, ½ inch (1.3 cm) wide (green)

12 inches (30.5 cm) satin ribbon, ⅛ inch (3 mm) wide (yellow)

Hand-sewing needle and thread

Straight pins

6 inches (15.2 cm) satin or grosgrain ribbon, ⅜ inch (9.5 mm) wide (green)

6 inches (15.2 cm) satin or grosgrain ribbon, 1 inch (2.5 cm) wide (green)

Adhesive-backed hook-and-loop circle, ½ inch (1.3 cm) in diameter

Metal loop

Carabiner

What You Do

1. Turn under 1 inch (2.5 cm) of one edge of the sturdy fabric, and stitch.

2. Cut both widths of the nylon webbing into 6-inch (15.2 cm) lengths. Cut the ⅛-inch-wide (3 mm) satin ribbon (yellow) into two 6-inch (15.2 cm) lengths.

3. Use a simple over-and-under technique to weave the pieces of nylon webbing. Run the narrow webbing vertically and the wide webbing horizontally. Tack or pin the ends of the webbing to hold the weave in place.

4. Weave the ⅛-inch-wide (3 mm) satin ribbons (yellow) through the woven webbing. Run one piece vertically and one piece horizontally. Add the ⅜-inch-wide (9.5 mm) satin or grosgrain ribbon (green) to the weaving, and then sew around the perimeter of the weaving, ¼ inch (6 mm) in from the edges.

5. Fold the 1-inch-wide (2.5 cm) piece of satin or grosgrain ribbon (green) over the top edge of the woven webbing, and stitch in place.

6. With the right sides together, stitch the piece of woven webbing to the sturdy fabric, leaving the top edge open. Turn the bag right side out, and push out the corners.

7. Cut a 2½-inch (6.4 cm) piece of the 1-inch-wide (2.5 cm) nylon webbing (navy) for the pouch closure. Stitch one end of this piece to the center of the inside top edge of the sturdy fabric. Turn under, and stitch a ¼-inch (6 mm) hem in the other end of the pouch closure. Affix one side of the adhesive-backed hook-and-loop circle under the hem of the pouch closure and the second circle in the center of the ribbon attached in step 5.

8. Cut a 2-inch (5 cm) piece of the ½-inch-wide (1.3 cm) nylon webbing (green). Feed one end of the webbing through the metal loop, fold the webbing in half, and then stitch it inside of one of the pouch's top corners. Hook the carabiner onto the loop.

DESIGNER
JOAN K. MORRIS

Graceful Pleats Tieback

Very wide ribbon makes this unique curtain tieback possible. Crisp double box pleats are sewn down the center to create the ruffle effect. Take your time selecting just the right buttons—they're essential to the overall look.

2 yards (1.8 m) fairly stiff wire-edge ribbon, such as taffeta, 4½ inches (11.4 cm) wide

Straight pins

Sewing machine

Invisible thread

Hand-sewing needle

½ yard (45.7 cm) decorative cord

6 buttons, each ½ inch (1.3 cm) in diameter

What You Do

1. Fold the length of ribbon in half to mark the center. Press the fold with your fingers to lightly crease it. Unfold the ribbon and lay it on a flat surface with the wrong side facing up.

2. Measure 1½ inches (3.8 cm) to one side of the center crease. Lightly crease the edge of the ribbon at that mark. Fold the ribbon end back over, and crease its width at that mark. Fold the ribbon length back over the crease you just made. Crease the ribbon width alongside the center crease. Repeat this step on the opposite side of the center crease. Secure the pleat with straight pins (see figure 1).

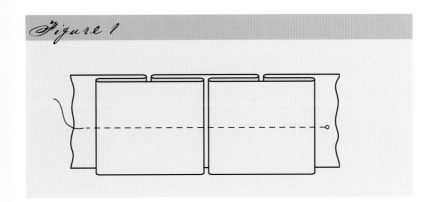

Figure 1

3. Turn over the ribbon, so the right side faces up. Measure 1½ inches (3.8 cm) from each crease. Crease the bottom edge. Fold the ribbon end toward the first pleat, and crease the ribbon alongside the first pleat. Repeat on the opposite side of the pleat. Pin the folds in place.

4. Turn over the ribbon, so the wrong side faces up. Measure over 1½ inches (3.8 cm) from the fold. Create a pleat as you did in step 3. Pin the pleat in place.

5. Create five full pleats on the right side of the ribbon. At each end, make a half pleat. Pin each in place.

6. Use invisible thread to machine-stitch down the center of the pleats. Do not stitch the free ends of the ribbon. Fold over ½ inch (1.3 cm) of ribbon at each end. Hand- or machine-stitch it in place to hem the cut edge. Turn over the pleated ribbon, so the wrong side faces up.

7. Cut the decorative cord in half. Pick up one length and fold it in half. Lay the folded cord on one end, allowing the loop to extend 2½ inches (6.4 cm) past the end of the ribbon. Fold the corners of the ribbon over the cord, creating a pointed end. Stitch the pointed end and cord in place by hand or machine. Repeat on the other end of the ribbon.

8. Bring over the loop end and crease it alongside the last crease on the wrong side. (You'll have made a full pleat on the front.) Pin it in place. Use the needle and matching thread to tack this fold in place at the top, center, and bottom. Repeat at the opposite end.

9. On the front of the tieback, hand-stitch each button on the edge of each pleat.

The
Ribbon Pull

In victorian England, traditional wedding festivities included a ribbon pull. The baker baked sterling silver charms into the wedding cake. Tied to elegant ribbons, each charm was a different shape and was symbolic of luck and good fortune. Prior to the newly-weds sharing their first slice of cake, the bridesmaids gathered around the dessert table. Each selected a ribbon to pull, and the connected amulet revealed her future. This charming ribbon ritual is still a part of many wedding celebrations.

Bamboo Lamp

DESIGNER
JOAN K. MORRIS

An Asian-themed jacquard ribbon paired with lustrous solid sheers makes this unique lighting fixture truly grand. Diffused by the ribbon, the bulb casts a rich glow of warm light. Bamboo, currently a popular craft material, is sold at many retail outlets such as art supply stores, home improvement and decorating centers, and garden shops.

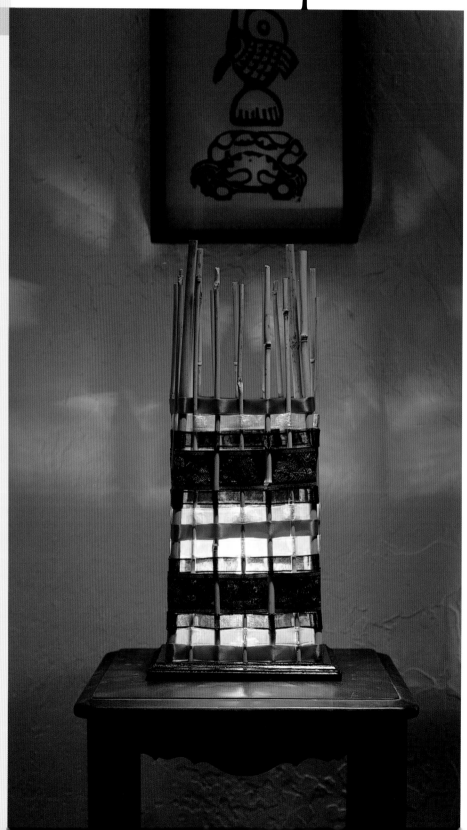

**9 x 7-inch (22.9 x 17.8 cm)
wood craft plaque
with beveled edges
for lamp base**

Drill

**2 drill bits, ¼ and ½ inch
(6 mm and 1.3 cm)
in diameter**

**4 bamboo sticks, ½ inch
(1.3 cm) in diameter, 20
inches (50.8 cm) long**

**8 bamboo sticks, ¼ inch
(6 mm) in diameter,
19 inches (48.3 cm) long**

**8 bamboo sticks, ¼ inch
(6 mm) in diameter,
18 inches (45.7 cm) long**

Utility knife

Sandpaper

Acrylic paint, black

Hot glue gun and glue sticks

Night-light kit

Wood glue

**1½ yards (1.4 m) jacquard
ribbon, 2 inches (5 cm) wide
(fish pattern)**

**2½ yards (2.3 m) satin
ribbon, 2½ inches (6.4 cm)
wide (red)**

**3½ yards (3.2 m) organdy
or mesh ribbon, 3 inches
(7.6 cm) wide (black)**

**3½ yards (3.2 m) organdy or
mesh ribbon, 3 inches
(7.6 cm) wide (gold)**

Straight pins

What You Do

1. Measure and mark four points at the corners of the wood base, each 1 inch (2.5 cm) in from the edges. Use the ½-inch (1.3 cm) bit to drill a hole at each point.

2. Measure and mark five equally spaced points down the length of, and 1-inch (2.5 cm) in from, the 9-inch (22.9 cm) side of the wood base. Use the ¼-inch (6 mm) bit to drill holes at these points.

3. Measure and mark three equally spaced points down the length of, and 1-inch (2.5 cm) in from, the 7-inch (17.8 cm) side of the wood base. Use the ¼-inch (6 mm) bit to drill holes at these points.

4. Test-fit the bamboo into each hole. Alternate the longer and shorter lengths of the ¼-inch (6 mm) bamboo. As needed, use a utility knife to whittle the ends of the bamboo to fit in the holes.

5. Sand the wood base, and then paint it with the black acrylic. Let dry.

6. Following the manufacturer's instructions, hot glue the night-light kit into the center of the painted wood base. Decide which of the 9-inch (22.9 cm) sides of the base will be the back of the lamp, and then run the night-light cord out between two drilled holes.

7. Use the wood glue to affix the bamboo sticks into the drilled holes. Let the glue dry.

8. Measure and cut all the ribbons into 30-inch (76.2 cm) lengths. This gives you two jacquard pieces, three satin pieces, four organdy or mesh pieces of one color (red), and four organdy or mesh pieces of a second color (gold).

9. Fold one piece of the satin ribbon (red) in half lengthwise. Weave it onto the lamp base so the ribbon is on the outside of the four bamboo corners. Pin the ribbon ends together in back of the lamp.

10. Fold one piece of the organdy or mesh ribbon (gold) in half lengthwise. Weave it onto the lamp base in the opposite direction of the previous layer (the ribbon is on the inside of the bamboo at the corners). Pin the ribbon ends together in back of the lamp.

11. Fold one piece of the organdy or mesh ribbon (black) in half lengthwise. Weave it onto the lamp base in the opposite direction of the previous layer. Pin the ribbon ends together in the back of the lamp.

12. Weave the jacquard ribbon into the bamboo opposite the previous layer, but keep the ribbon on the outside of the four bamboo corners to better show the pattern. Pin the ribbon ends in back.

13. Invent your own design or use the following sequence of woven ribbon layers to recreate the lamp pictured: organdy or mesh (black); organdy or mesh (gold); satin (red); organdy or mesh (gold); organdy or mesh (black); jacquard; organdy or mesh (black); organdy or mesh (gold); and satin (red). This gives you a total of 13 woven ribbon layers.

14. Once you're satisfied with the weaving, hot glue the ribbon ends together on the back side of the lamp , and remove the pins.

Imperial Pillow

DESIGNER

JOAN K. MORRIS

*Here's your chance
to collect a regal array
of ribbons and compose
them into a stately
work of art. Perfectly
coordinated, the
ribbons resemble
a single piece of
fabric instead of a
simple sampler.
Blend satins, sheers,
metallics, taffettas,
and embroidered ribbon
to create your own
classic cushion.*

1 yard (.9 m) each of eight or more complementary-colored ribbons in different widths and textures

Sewing machine with a zigzag setting and a zipper foot

Matching or invisible thread

¾ yard (68.6 cm) complementary-colored fabric for pillow back

2 yards (1.8 m) lip cord (trim with a lip)

Straight pins

16 x 12-inch (40.6 x 30.5 cm) pillow form

Hand-sewing needle

What You Do

1. Measure and cut each ribbon into two 13-inch (33 cm) lengths.

2. Lay out the ribbons edge to edge in an attractive arrangement that is 17 inches (43.2 cm) wide. Machine- or hand-stitch the edges of the ribbons together using a zigzag stitch.

3. Measure and cut the pillow back fabric into a 13 x 17-inch (33 x 43.1 cm) rectangle.

4. Use the zipper foot on the sewing machine to baste the lip cord to the right side of the pillow back fabric. Match the lip of the cord to the edge of the fabric.

5. Position the stitched ribbons (the pillow front) right sides together with the trimmed pillow back fabric, and pin. Use the zipper foot on the sewing machine to stitch the front and back sides of the pillow together, leaving a 6- to 8-inch (15.2 to 20.3 cm) opening.

6. Turn the stitched fabric right side out, and push out the corners. Carefully stuff the pillow form into the pillow cover, and hand-stitch closed.

Mediterranean
Message Board

DESIGNER
JOAN K. MORRIS

If you want to display postcards, children's drawings, grocery lists, and invitations but find ordinary cork bulletin boards a bit dreary, this custom-designed upholstered board is the solution. Precious papers tuck behind criss-crossed ribbons for safe and stylish storage.

WHAT YOU NEED

**8-foot (2.4 m) piece of
1 x 1-inch (2.5 x 2.5 cm)
wood**

Saw

Hammer

Nails

**Foam-core board, ½ inch
(1.3 cm) thick***

Silicon glue

Spray adhesive

**20 x 25-inch (50.8 x 63.5
cm) piece of quilting batting**

**1 yard (.9 m) upholstery
fabric**

Staple gun and staples

**7 yards (6.4 m) cut-edge
ribbon, 2½ inches (6.4 cm)
wide**

Iron

Straight pins

**Large hand-sewing needle
and strong thread**

Upholstery tacks

Fabric glue

*Foam-core board is made of
two layers of smooth card
stock laminated over a layer
of polystyrene. White and
black foam-core boards are
commonly sold at craft and
office supply stores.

What You Do

1. Cut the wood into four pieces. Cut two pieces 20 inches (50.8 cm) long, and cut two pieces 25 inches (63.5 cm) long. Miter the ends of the cut wood to make corner angles. Use a hammer and nails to create a 20 x 25 inch (50.8 x 63.5 cm) wood frame.

2. Measure, mark, and cut the foam-core board into a 20 x 25-inch (50.8 x 63.5 cm) rectangle. Attach the foam-core to the wood frame with the silicon glue. Using the spray adhesive, attach the quilting batting to the front of the foam-core board.

3. Center the upholstery fabric over the batting with its right side facing out. Tightly pull the fabric over the frame. Staple the fabric to the inside of the frame, placing the staples about 1 inch (2.5 cm) apart.

4. Cut three pieces of the cut-edge ribbon, each 30 inches (76.2 cm) long. Cut each of the 30-inch (76.2 cm) ribbons in half lengthwise, making six 30-inch (76.2 cm) ribbons. Fold each of the ribbons lengthwise into thirds with the edges meeting in the rear and the right side of the ribbon facing out. Use an iron to press the folded ribbons. Each piece is now ½ inch (1.3 cm) wide.

5. Take two of the folded ribbons and cross them at the center, forming an X shape. Pin the center of the X in the center of the fabric-covered board.

6. Cross two more ribbons and pin their center 8 inches (20.3 cm) to the left of the center of the ribbon X applied in step 5. Cross two more ribbons and pin their center 8 inches (20.3 cm) to the right of the center of the ribbon X applied in step 5.

7. Pull the ends of the outside ribbons to the top edge of the bulletin board and pin them behind the frame, one in each corner. From the

top left corner, measure over 8 inches (20.3 cm), and pin the next two ribbon ends at this point. Measure 8 inches (20.3 cm) more, and pin the next two ribbons.

8. Repeat step 7 for the bottom edge of the bulletin board. Use the staple gun to tightly and permanently secure all of the pinned ribbons to the inside of the wood frame.

9. At the center point of each ribbon X, insert a threaded needle and tightly pull it to create a tuft in the padded fabric. Attach one upholstery tack at the center of each ribbon X and on the top and

bottom board edges where two ribbons intersect.

10. Cut two 1-yard (.9 m) pieces of the remaining ribbon. Fold the ribbon in half lengthwise, with the right side facing out, and bind with fabric glue.
Let dry.

11. Use the staple gun to attach one end of each ribbon to one inside corner at the top of the frame. Tie a bow with the loose ends of the hanging ribbons. Trim the ends of the ribbons as needed.

The Stephana

Ribbon plays an important role in Greek Orthodox weddings. One of the most important and powerful symbols of marriage, the *stephana* is a pair of individual crowns connected by a ribbon signifying unity. During the ceremony, the stephana is placed on the heads of the bride and groom. The elegant crowns are cherished by the couple and placed in the home altar or in a special case called a *stephanothiki*.

Scarf *Seduction*

DESIGNER
ELIZABETH HELENE SEARLE

Shimmering and alluring, this wearable piece of art features an intriguing mixture of straight and curved ribbons that peek through sheer chiffon. Textures abound as the layers of luxurious silk and chiffon are cut at angles, becoming part of the scarf sculpture and revealing the ribbon.

1½ yards (1.4 m) silk
duppioni

1½ yards (1.4 m) silk
chiffon or organza

Tailor's chalk

3 yards (2.7 m) bias-cut
silk ribbon, 1⅜ inches
(3.5 cm) wide

5 or more yards (4.6 m)
sheer ribbon, ½ inch
(1.3 cm) wide

Thread

Sewing machine with
quilting guide

Iron

What You Do

1. Remove the selvage edge from the silk fabrics. On the straight of the grain, cut two 1½-yard x 14-inch (1.4 m x 35.6 cm) pieces of silk, one from each of the fabrics.

2. Lay the silk duppioni flat on your work surface. Use the tailor's chalk to mark a succession of parallel lines across the fabric, slanting the lines at a 45° angle to the bottom long edge of the fabric (see figure 1).

3. Cut the bias-cut silk ribbon to fit on top of the chalk lines marked in step 2. Position the ribbons on top of the fabric. Arrange the sheer ribbon over the bias-cut silk ribbon in a random squiggle pattern, as shown in figure 1.

Figure 1

4. Carefully place the chiffon or organza over the duppioni, sandwiching the ribbons. Pin heavily to hold the silks and ribbons in place.

5. At one corner of the fabric, use the chalk to mark a line that intersects the ribbon; then machine-stitch across the marked line.

6. Using the sewing machine's quilting guide, stitch parallel lines that are ¾ inch (1.9 cm) apart across the length of the scarf. Always stitch on the bias, and check every few rows to see that the stitches remain at a 45° angle. (Because you're stitching on the bias, your stitches may become curved. You can compensate for curved stitches by making the rows slightly more narrow as needed.) Completely cover the scarf with rows of stitching.

7. On one side of the fabric, cut through the top layer of fabric at every other row. Turn over the scarf, and cut through the top layer of fabric at every row that wasn't cut on the other side. (If you cut the wrong row, you'll cut the scarf apart, so you might want to mark the rows with a straight pin or chalk before cutting.)

8. With an iron, press all the cut edges in one direction. Turn over the scarf, and use an iron to press all the cut edges in the opposite direction.

9. Trim threads and straighten jagged edges as needed. Top-stitch around the scarf ½ inch (1.3 cm) in from the edge.

The
Ribbon Dance

The Ribbon Dance, or Red Silk Dance, is one of the most popular folk dances in China. It was created during imperial times by the Han, China's largest ethnic group. It's a commonly held belief that the dance was first performed to honor a faithful servant who defended his master with the long-flowing sleeves of his gown. The modern dance uses a pair of long colorful ribbons attached to poles or held directly in the dancer's hands. The dancers use the ribbons to create elegant and expressive movements. A sensational display of color and energy, the Ribbon Dance is often performed at festivals and celebrations.

DESIGNER
BARBARA ZARETSKY

Heavenly Table Topper

You might expect angels to gather round your table once you create this runner from ivory silk, sheer ribbons, and delicate seed beads. This luminous linen is the perfect accent for a bridal shower, dinner party, or other elegant affair.

2 pieces of fabric, each 15½ x 71 inches (39.4 x 180.3 cm)

Straight pins

2 pieces of sheer ribbon, each 71 inches (180.3 cm) long, 1⅜ inches (3.5 cm) wide

Sewing machine or hand-sewing needle and thread

2 pieces of sheer ribbon, each 15½ inches (39.4 cm) long, 1⅜ inches (3.5 cm) wide

Seed beads

Beading needle and thread

Iron

What You Do

1. Take one piece of the 15½ x 71-inch (39.4 x 180.3 cm) fabric and measure in 2½ inches (6.4 cm) from the edges. Mark with pins.

2. Lay the long ribbon pieces adjacent to the guide pins. Pin the ribbons in place, and then remove the guide pins. Stitch down both sides of the long ribbons, staying very close to their edges. Remove the pins.

3. Repeat steps 1 and 2 for the short edges of the fabric. The short ribbons overlap the long ribbon lengths.

4. Use the beading needle to string 1 inch (2.5 cm) of seed beads on the beading thread. Use a couching stitch (see figure 1) to sew the seed beads diagonally across the square formed by the intersection of the long and short ribbons. (This intersection occurs near all four corners of the cloth.) Make sure all the rows of beads run in the same direction.

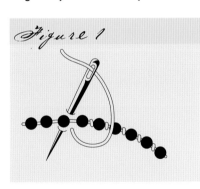

Figure 1

5. Lay the embellished fabric face up on your work surface. Place the second piece of fabric on top with its right side down. Pin the two pieces of fabric together.

6. Using a ½-inch (1.3 cm) seam allowance, stitch the two pieces of fabric together, leaving a 5-inch (12.7 cm) opening.

7. Turn the sewn fabric right side out. Use an iron to press the seams. Turn in the unsewn opening edges ½ inch (1.3 cm) to match the seam allowance. Stitch the opening closed with an invisible slip stitch (see page 91). Press the table runner.

Drawstring Purse

DESIGNER
ELIZABETH HELENE SEARLE

When you're traveling light for a night out on the town—just carrying lipstick and a compact perhaps—reach for this elegant drawstring purse. It's the perfect evening accessory. Use your favorite fabric, flowers, and lining to create a one-of-a-kind fashion accent.

WHAT YOU NEED

½ yard (45.7 cm) purse fabric, 45 inches (114.3 cm) wide

Tailor's chalk

Cup or plate

¼ yard (22.9 cm) lining fabric

2 yards (1.8 m) narrow cording for drawstring

1½ yard (1.4 m) wire-edge ribbon, 1½ inches (3.8 cm) wide (for roses)

10 inches (25.4 cm) wire-edge ribbon, 1½ inches (3.8 cm) wide (for leaves)

What You Do

1. Cut two pieces of the purse fabric, each 10 x 13 inches (25.4 x 33 cm). Using the cup or plate as a guide to make consistent curves, mark where you'll round off the corners of the fabric with chalk (see figure 1). Trim the fabric along the marked lines.

2. Cut two pieces of the lining fabric, each 10 x 7½ inches (25.4 x 19 cm). Round off the corners of the fabric using the same method described in step 1. Make sure the curves for the purse fabric and the lining are the same.

3. Using a ¼-inch (6 mm) seam allowance, sew the right side of the purse fabric to the lining. Leave an opening in the lining so the fabric can be turned. Press the seam toward the lining. Leave two 1¼-inch (3.2 cm) openings for the casing 5¼ inches (13.3 cm) down from the top of the stitched bag. Turn the bag right side out, press, and then push the lining inside. The purse fabric partially will turn inside the bag, approximately 2½ inches (6.4 cm) from the top.

4. To make the casing, hand-stitch around the bag 2¼ inches (5.7 cm) from the top, and then 3½ inches (8.9 cm) from the top. Run the cording through the casing from each side, and knot the ends.

5. Create the rose and leaves following the basic directions found on pages 19 and 20. Stitch the ribbon flowers to the top of the purse.

Figure 1

Nursery Cubbies

DESIGNER

JOAN K. MORRIS

When decorating today's nursery, you need not stick to subdued pastel colors. Let the vibrant fabric and woven ribbon patterns of this all-in-one organizer capture your baby's attention and save you time at the changing station.

WHAT YOU NEED

1 yard (.9 m) background fabric

3 yards (2.7 m) fusible interfacing

Iron and ironing board

5 different pocket fabrics, fat quarters or remnants*

5 double-faced satin ribbons, 3 yards (2.7 m) each, ¼ inch (6 mm) wide, in five different colors (orange, pink, fuschia, blue, and yellow)

Straight pins

Invisible thread

Sewing machine with a zigzag setting

Hand-sewing needle and thread

1 yard (.9 m) sheer wire-edge ribbon (polka dot)

*A *fat quarter* refers to the method of cutting a quarter of 1 yard (.9 m) of fabric from a bolt of cloth. If you were to roll out and cut 9 inches (22.9 cm) of fabric from a bolt, you'd end up with a narrow strip. However, if you roll out 1 yard (.9 m) and cut that amount into quarters, the result is a more useful, nearly square piece of fabric.

What You Do

1. Cut two pieces of the background fabric, each 25 x 31 inches (63.5 x 78.7 cm). Cut a 24 x 30-inch (60.9 x 76.2 cm) piece of fusible interfacing. Center the fusible interfacing on top of one piece of the background fabric. Following the manufacturer's instructions, join the interfacing to one piece of the background fabric.

2. Select two of the pocket fabrics. Cut out two 9 x 9-inch (22.9 x 22.9 cm) squares from each of the fabrics. Cut out two 7 x 8-inch (17.8 x 20.3 cm) squares from each of the three remaining pocket fabrics.

3. Select two colors of the ¼-inch-wide (6 mm) satin ribbons to use for each pocket. Cut a total of 24 pieces, 6 inches (15.2 cm) in length, for every color of pocket ribbon.

4. On top of the ironing board, line up one color of ribbon vertically with all edges flush. Pin the end of each ribbon on its right side. (Stick the pin through the ribbon and into the ironing board at a 45° angle, as shown in figure 1a.)

5. Starting at the top right edge of the ribbons pinned in step 4, pin one piece of the second ribbon color horizontally into the ironing board.

Figure 1

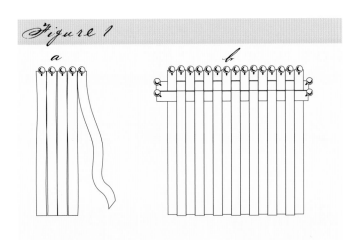

a

b

121

6. Weave the horizontal ribbon over and under the 24 pinned ribbons; then pin the left end of the ribbon to the ironing board (see figure 1b). Continue this weaving process using each of the 24 remaining ribbon pieces and pinning each at the left and right. (Alternate the weaving pattern so one ribbon winds over then under, while the next is under then over, and so on.) Carefully remove the straight pins from the ribbons and ironing board.

7. Cut a 6 x 6-inch (15.2 x 15.2 cm) piece of fusible interfacing. Following the manufacturer's directions, fuse the interfacing to the woven ribbon.

8. Repeat steps 4 through 7 to weave and fuse each set of pocket ribbons.

9. Draw five simple shapes, one for each pocket. Each design must fit within the 6 x 6-inch (15.2 x 15.2 cm) square of fused woven ribbon. (This design uses a diamond, square, circle, heart, and flower.)

10. Transfer one of the shapes onto one of the fused woven ribbon squares and carefully cut it out. Place the shape onto one of the fabric pockets. Using invisible thread, machine-stitch the shape to the pocket, staying close to the edge. Switch the sewing machine to a zigzag stitch, and sew around the shape again.

11. Repeat step 10 for each shape and pocket. If you have any problems with fraying, you may want to stitch a piece of ribbon around the edge of the shape. (In this design, a ribbon is stitched around the diamond shape.)

12. Cut two pieces of fusible interfacing, each 8 x 8 inches (20.3 x 20.3 cm). Cut three pieces of fusible interfacing, each 6 x 7 inches (15.2 x 17.8 cm).

13. Center one piece of 8 x 8-inch (20.3 x 20.3 cm) fusible interfacing onto the wrong side of one 9 x 9-inch (22.9 x 22.9 cm) ribbon-embellished pocket. Fuse the interfacing to the wrong side of the pocket.

14. Repeat step 13 on the remaining decorated 9 x 9-inch (22.9 x 22.9 cm) pocket and the three decorated 7 x 8-inch (17.8 x 20.3 cm) pockets.

15. Assemble the decorated and plain pieces of fabric for each pocket. Place their right sides together. Using a ½-inch (1.3 cm) seam allowance, sew around each pocket, leaving a 3-inch (7.6 cm) opening in the bottom edge. Clip the corners of the fabric and turn the pockets right side out, making sure the corners are completely pushed out. Use an iron to press each pocket flat. Hand-stitch each pocket closed, turning in the fabric ½ inch (1.3 cm) to match the seam allowance.

16. Pin the pockets onto the front piece of the background fabric. [In this design, the larger two pockets are both 4½ inches (11.4 cm) in from the side edges and 2½ inches (6.4 cm) up from the bottom edge of the background fabric. Two of the smaller pockets are 5 inches (12.7 cm) down from the top edge of the fabric and 4 inches (10.2 cm) in from the side edges. The fifth pocket is centered below and between the top two pockets.] Leaving the top edges open, machine-stitch the pockets onto the fabric with invisible thread.

17. Cut three pieces of the sheer wire-edge ribbon (polka dot), each 8 inches (20.3 cm) long. Fold each piece of cut ribbon in half. Center one folded ribbon near the top edge of the fabric's back side with its cut ends down, and pin in place. Position the other two folded ribbons on the back side of the fabric, 2 inches (5 cm) in from each side edge. Pin in place.

18. Place the two pieces of the background fabric together with their right sides facing. Using a ½-inch (1.3 cm) seam allowance, machine-stitch around the fabric, leaving a 6-inch (15.2 cm) opening in the bottom edge.

19. Turn the fabric right side out, push out the corners, and press flat. Hand-stitch the bottom edge closed, turning in the open edges ½ inch (1.3 cm) to match the seam allowance.

Contributing Designers

Julie Bell enjoys creating handmade gifts and home decorations for her family and friends from her home in Knoxville, Tennessee. Julie grew up in Asheville, North Carolina, and received a degree in Fashion Merchandising from the University of Georgia.

Sally Bryenton has maintained a working art studio in Western North Carolina for 25 years. She works primarily as an enamelist, mural painter, and decorative artist. Sewing was a skill Sally learned early. She has often designed and created textile items to include in her decorative painting projects.

Terry Taylor is a mixed media artist whose work has been shown in numerous exhibitions. He is a full-time employee of Lark Books.

Jen Hamilton and **Kate Kohn** are artists who live and work in Asheville, North Carolina.

Marvis Lutz and her husband, Keith, own The Button Embroidery & Ribbonry in Portland, Oregon. Marvis has enjoyed sewing, knitting, and embroidering since childhood. The store has become her creative outlet for teaching ribbon work and other fiber-related classes. Her true love is creating cloth art dolls and designing patterns.

Joan K. Morris' artistic endeavors have led her down many successful creative paths. A childhood interest in sewing turned into professional costuming for motion pictures. After studying ceramics, Joan ran her own clay wind chime business for 15 years. Since 1993 her coffeehouse, Vincent's Ear, has provided a vital meeting place for all varieties of artists and thinkers. She has created projects for numerous Lark books, including *Gifts for Baby* (2003) and *Weekend Crafter: Dried Flower Crafting* (2003).

Darla Owen is a floral designer with 25 years of experience. She first learned floral design from her mother; her parents have been involved in the floral industry for the past 33 years. Darla owned her own floral shop and has also worked for several florists. She's currently designing and doing freelance work in Asheville, North Carolina. Darla is also a professional archer; she's won seven world championships. Married for 23 years, Darla has two daughters and one grandson.

Elizabeth Helene Searle is a popular sewing instructor and custom clothing designer. Attractive, imaginative use of ribbon flowers is a trademark of her company, Elizabeth Helene Custom Designs, in Asheville, North Carolina.

Allison Smith has a home-based business specializing in providing deluxe tourist accommodations in remote locations in western North Carolina. She is also an avid crafter and designer in addition to being a full-time mother. She has created projects for numerous Lark books, including *Decorating Baskets* (2002), *Girls' World* (2000), and *Decorating Candles* (2002). She lives in Asheville, North Carolina.

Nicole Tuggle is a mixed-media artist whose recent work has focused on collage and assemblage constructions. She finds beauty in found objects and old, neglected treasures. Check out more of her work at: http://www.sigilation.com.

Barbara Zaretsky has been using a warm and earthy palette to create beautiful wearable textile art for more than 15 years. She specializes in hats and scarves. Barbara's work has been featured at numerous boutiques and craft shows. She studied textile design at Northern Illinois University and The Art Institute of Chicago.

Acknowledgments

I had the good fortune to work with an incredibly talented team of project designers. Thanks for your commitment to creativity, quality, and joy.

Thanks to Liz Cambridge of The Ribbon Club, Sheila Rolfer of Renaissance Ribbons, and Marvis and Keith Lutz of The Button Embroidery & Ribbonry for their dedication to promoting and generosity in providing exquisitely beautiful ribbons.

Thanks to Susan McBride and Michael Murphy, Keith and Wendy Wright, Betty Ashworth, and Rick Morris for providing photography locations and props.

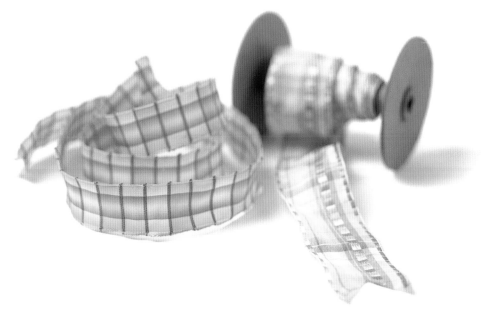

A Note About Suppliers

Usually, the supplies you need for making the projects in Lark books can be found at your local craft supply store, discount mart, home improvement center, or retail shop relevant to the topic of the book. Occasionally, however, you may need to buy materials or tools from specialty suppliers. In order to provide you with the most up-to-date information, we have created a listing of suppliers on our Web site, which we update on a regular basis. Visit us at www.larkbooks.com, click on "Craft Supply Sources," and then click on the relevant topic. You will find numerous companies listed with their Web address and/or mailing address and phone number.

Index

Adhesives, 16
Bedding & pillow projects
    Buttercup & Gingham
    Linens, 50
    Imperial Pillow, 107
    Open-Weave Pillows &
    Blanket, 56
    Tapestry Pillow, 70
Couching stitch, 117
Cut-edge ribbons, 9
Clothing & accessory projects
    Beautiful Borders, 38
    Drawstring Purse, 118
    Folded Flower Pin, 54
    Perfect Vision Valet, 80
    Scarf Seduction, 112
    Summer Sun Hat, 78
    Sun, Sand & Sea Tote, 30
    Travel Pouch, 98
Fork-cut ends, 18
Fray retardant, 18
Fusibles, 16
Gift wrap projects
    24-Karat Bow, 44
    Azure Fields Bow, 46
    Handcrafted Cards, 62
    Keepsake Gift Bag, 82

Grosgrain, 11
Hand-sewing needles, 16
Home decor projects
    Bamboo Lamp, 104
    Button & Bow Candle, 34
    Glamour Shade, 74
    Mediterranean Message
    Board, 109
    Nursery Cubbies, 120
    Periwinkle Passion
Wreath, 96
    Picture Perfect Wall
Hanging, 87
    Pleased-to-Meet-You Mat,
    72
    Trace of Taffeta Wreath, 76
    Versatile Orbs, 32
    Woven Picture Frame, 48
    Zesty Mosaic Tray, 26
Jacquard, 11
Jumping the Broom, 67
Keepsake & heirloom
projects
    Beaded Bookmark, 36
    Heart-to-Heart Sachet, 66
    Pin Pillow, 93
    Silky Lingerie Bag, 84
    Snapshot Scrapbook, 68

Markers, 18
Metallic, 12
Odds and ends, 18
Organdy, 12
Ombré, 12
Picot-edge ribbon, 10
Pointed flower petals, 20
Removing wire, 18
Ribbon leaf, 20
Ribbon storage, 15
Ribbon width, 14
Satin, 13
Scissors, 16
Sewing machines, 17
Slip stitch, 91
Table linen projects
    Celestial Cloth, 60
    Chopstick Pocket, 42
    Heavenly Table Topper,
    116
    Linen Place Mat &
    Napkin, 90
    No-Sew Chic Napkin
    Rings, 24
    Table Rays, 58
Taffeta, 13
The Eve of St. Andrews, 59
The Maypole, 21

The Ribbon Dance, 115
The Ribbon Pull, 103
The Sneud, 95
The Stephana, 111
Threads, 17
Velvet, 13
Window treatment projects
    Graceful Pleats Tieback,
    100
    Rosy Ruffled Shade, 52
    Sheer Bliss, 28
    Supernova Shade, 40
Wire-edge ribbons, 10
Wired ribbon rose, 19
Woven-edge ribbons, 10

My name is

. . . .

Notes for parents and teachers

This book develops and extends early concepts of *adding and subtracting* for adults and children to enjoy and share together. It has been carefully written to introduce key words and ideas that children will meet in their first couple of years in school.

Throughout the book, you will see **Word Banks** that contain the new math terms introduced for each concept. All the words from the word banks are gathered together at the back of the book. You can use the word banks with your child in several ways:

- See which of the words they recognized through games such as *I spy. I spy the word "plus"—can you find it? I spy a word beginning with "m"—where is it?*
- Choose a word and ask your child to find it in the book.
- Let your child choose a word and say something about it.

Look for other opportunities in everyday life to use the ideas and vocabulary introduced in this book. Add up sums of money, count how many knives and forks there are altogether, or total dice scores. Make sure your child realizes that addition and subtraction are easy, and most importantly, fun.

Adding and totaling

Putting sets together is the same as adding. This sign means add **+**.

Adding makes a set larger.

 **+**

Altogether there are

3 ladybugs   2 bees   5 insects.

 **+**

Altogether there are

4 green planets   3 purple planets   7 planets.

 **+**

6 add 4 makes 10.

4

What is the total number of birds? 8

What is the total number of ice creams? 8

Word Bank

count

add

altogether

total

makes

more

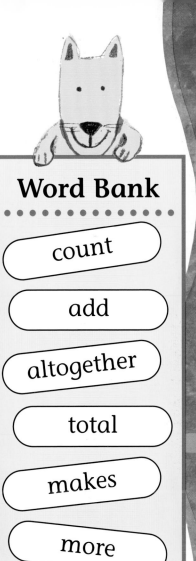

What is the total number of dinosaurs? 9

Taking away and subtracting

Taking away is the same as subtracting.
This sign means subtract ─ .

Taking away makes a set smaller.

5 take away 2 leaves 3.

6 remove 1 leaves 5. 4

8 take away 2 leaves 6. 6

9 subtract 3 leaves 6. 6

How many have left the bowl? 5
How many have stayed behind? 3

How many are leaving? 4
How many are staying behind? 6

2 ducks fly away.
How many will be left? 4

3 fish are eaten.
How many will that leave? 2

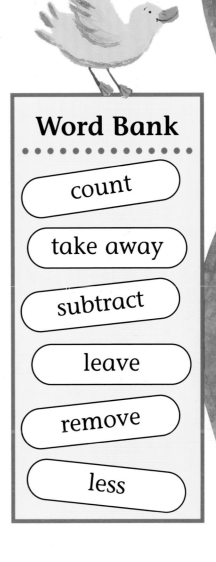

How many more?

Comparing sets tells us which one has more.

You can find out how many more by counting ahead.
Count ahead from the smaller number.

5 is 2 more than 3.

4 is 2 more than 2.

7 is 3 more than 4.

There are more purple snails than green snails. There are 3 more.

5 green snails

8 purple snails

Tom

Who has more bricks?
How many more?

Joe

Who has made the longer line?
How many more are needed to make
them the same?

10

7

Fran

Ben

Who has the higher score?
How many more?

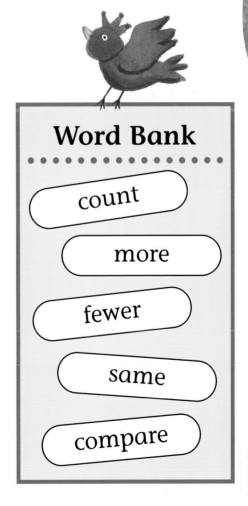

Word Bank

count

more

fewer

same

compare

Jumping along and adding

We can use a number track
to help with adding.

Jumping forward along a number
track is the same as adding on.

Frog was on 5 and jumped forward 2.

5 + 2 makes 7

Frog is on 3. She will make 4 jumps.

3 + 4 makes 7

Frog is on 6. To reach 10 she must
make 4 jumps.

6 + 4 makes 10

3 + 2

Where do you start?
How many jumps?
Where do you end?

5 + 4

Where do you start?
How many jumps?
Where do you end?

Start on 4.
Jump to 10.
How many jumps?

Word Bank

count ahead
makes
add
forward

11

Jumping back and subtracting

We can use a number track to help with subtracting.

Jumping back along a number track is the same as subtracting or taking away.

Bee started on 5 and jumped back 2.

5 – 2 leaves 3

Bee was on 7. She made 4 jumps back.

7 – 4 is 3

Bee is on 10. To reach 4 she must make 6 jumps.

10 – 6 reaches 4

6 – 4

Where do you start?
How many jumps?
Where do you end?

10 – 6

Where do you start?
How many jumps?
Where do you end?

Start on 9.
Jump to 4.
How many jumps?

Plus and equals

We use these two signs when we are adding, **+** and **=** .

+ is the plus sign.   **=** is the equals sign.

The plus sign tells us to add.

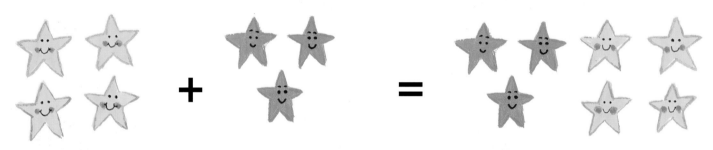

Four plus three equals seven.

$$4 + 3 = 7$$

Two and seven more makes nine.

$$2 + 7 = 9$$

Three jump along five reaches eight.

$$3 + 5 = 8$$

$$3 + 5 = 8 \text{ is a sum}$$

14

$$3 + 5 = 8$$

$$5 + 3 = 8$$

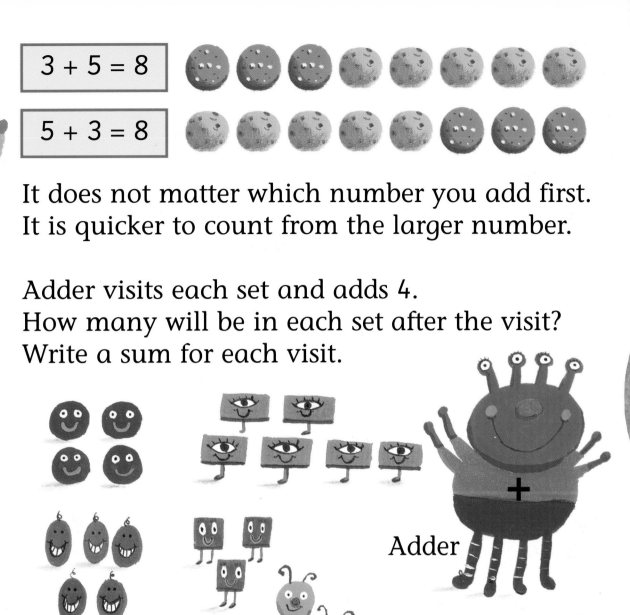

It does not matter which number you add first.
It is quicker to count from the larger number.

Adder visits each set and adds 4.
How many will be in each set after the visit?
Write a sum for each visit.

Adder

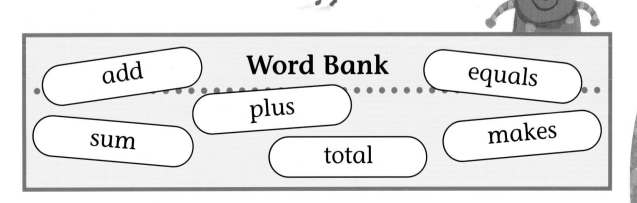

	Word Bank	
add		equals
	plus	
sum		makes
	total	

Minus and equals

We use these two signs when we are subtracting, — and = .

— is the minus sign.   = is the equals sign.

The minus sign tells us to subtract.

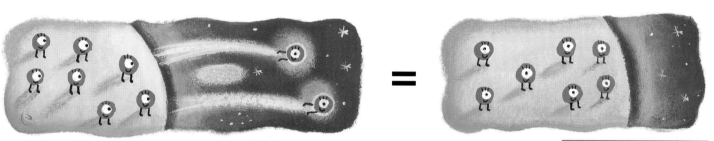

Nine take away two   equals seven.

$$9 - 2 = 7$$

Six take away two   equals four.

$$6 - 2 = 4$$

Ten jump back four is six.

$$10 - 4 = 6$$

$10 - 4 = 6$ is a subtraction

Counting back can help us subtract.

$$6 - 4 = 2$$

6 count back 4 lands on 2.

Nipper visits each set and takes away 4.
How many will be in each set after the visit?
Write a subtraction sum for each visit.

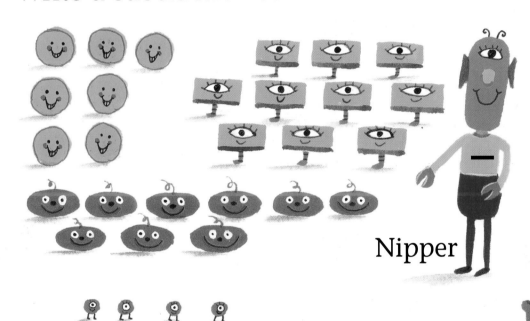

Nipper

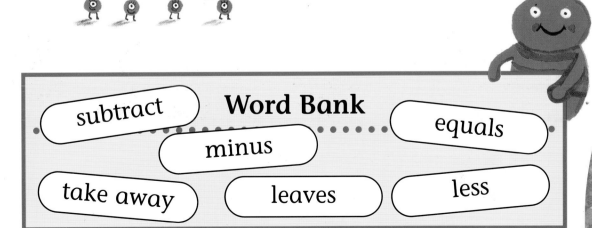

Word Bank

subtract

minus

equals

take away   leaves   less

10
9
8
7
6
5
4
3
2
1

Adding machines

Number machines change numbers.
Adding machines make numbers larger.

Numbers go into the adding machine.
The machine changes the number.
The answer comes out of the machine.

4 enters the machine.
It adds on 3.
7 will leave the machine.

2 enters the machine.
It adds on 4.
6 will leave the machine.

18

Jumping along the number track will help you add on.

| 0 | 1 | 2 | 3 | 4 | 5 | 6 | 7 | 8 | 9 | 10 |

Which numbers will leave each of these machines?

Word Bank

add   equals

enter   total   leave   plus

Subtraction machines

Number machines change numbers.
Subtraction machines make numbers smaller.

Numbers go into the take away machine.
The machine changes the number.
The answer comes out of the machine.

4 enters the machine.
It takes away 1.
3 will leave the machine.

5 enters the machine.
It takes away 2.
3 will leave the machine.

Jumping back on the number track will help you subtract.

0 1 2 3 4 5 6 7 8 9 10

Which numbers will leave each of these machines?

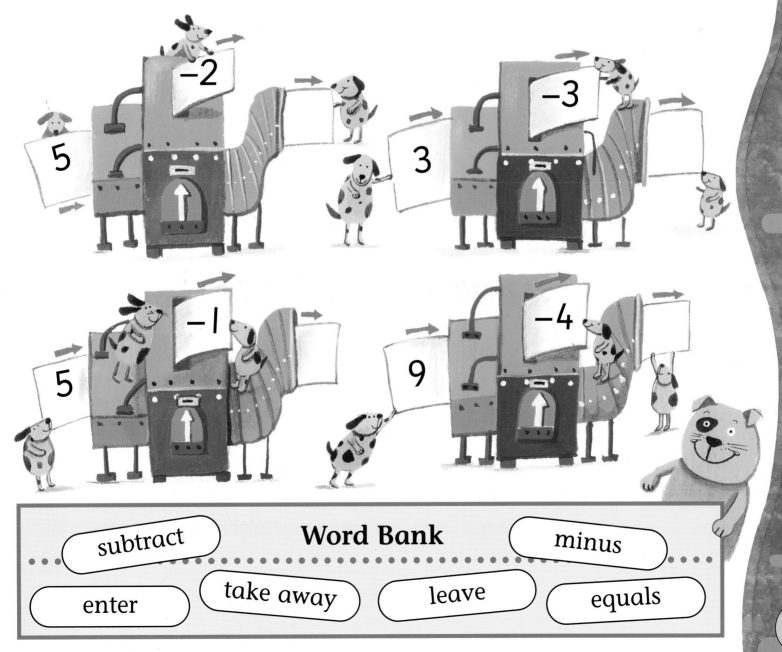

The story of 10

Pairs of numbers that add up to 10 are very important.

$1 + 9 = 10$

$2 + 8 = 10$

$3 + 7 = 10$

$4 + 6 = 10$

$5 + 5 = 10$

$6 + 4 = 10$

$7 + 3 = 10$

$8 + 2 = 10$

$9 + 1 = 10$

$10 + 0 = 10$

22

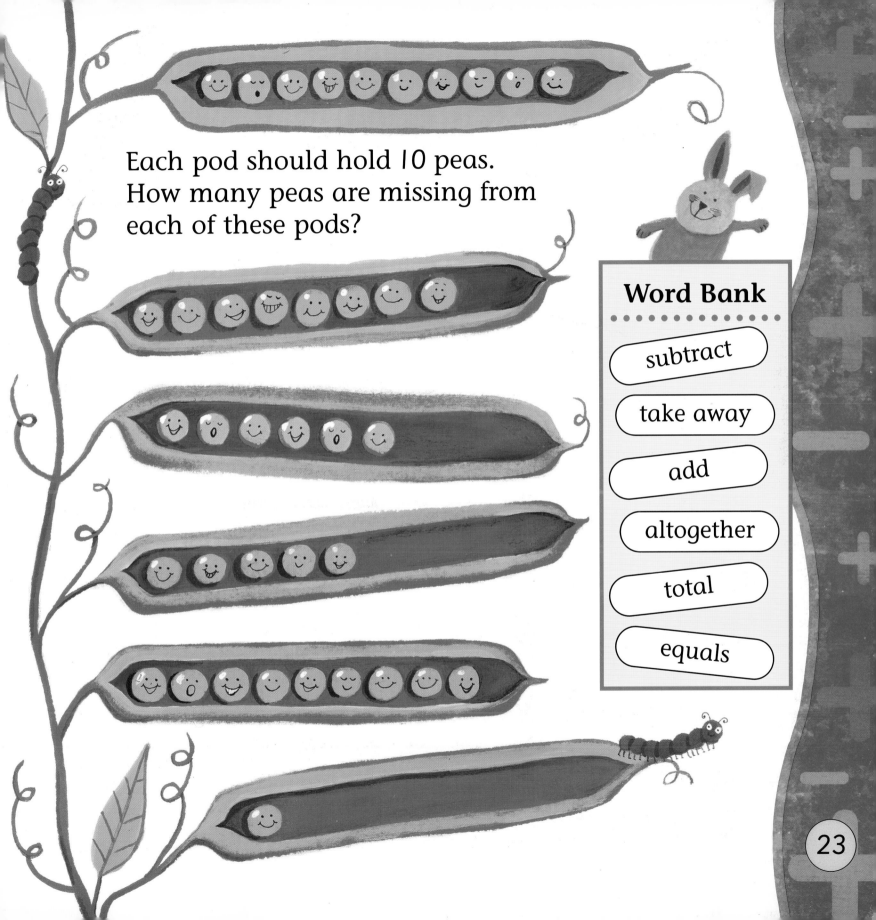

Each pod should hold 10 peas.
How many peas are missing from
each of these pods?

Word Bank

subtract

take away

add

altogether

total

equals

23

Counting ahead and back

We can add to large numbers.
Counting ahead will find the total.
We can subtract from large numbers.
Counting back will find the answer.

1 2 3 4 5 6 7 8 9 10

20 19 18 17 16 15 14 13 12 11

12 + 2 =		17 − 2 =

Start on 12.
Make 2 jumps forward.
You land on 14.
12 + 2 = 14

Start on 17.
Make 2 jumps back.
You land on 15.
17 − 2 = 15

Jumping forward is
the same as adding.

Jumping back is the
same as subtracting.

24

Use the number track to help you add and subtract.

Add on 2 to each of these numbers.

16   10   12   13   18

Subtract 3 from each of these numbers.

17   13   15   16   20

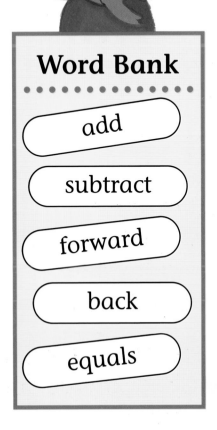

Word Bank
· · · · · · · · · · · · · · · ·

add

subtract

forward

back

equals

25

Using zero

Zero is the number 0.
We sometimes call it nought or nothing.

Adding zero, or nothing, to any number does not change it.

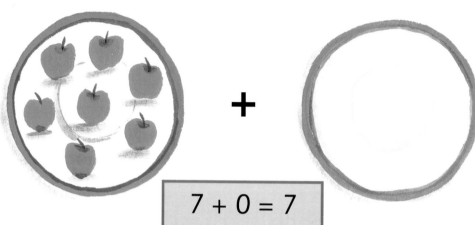

$$7 + 0 = 7$$

Subtracting zero, or nothing, from any number does not change it.

$$5 - 0 = 5$$

Word Bank

zero

adding

nought

nothing

subtracting

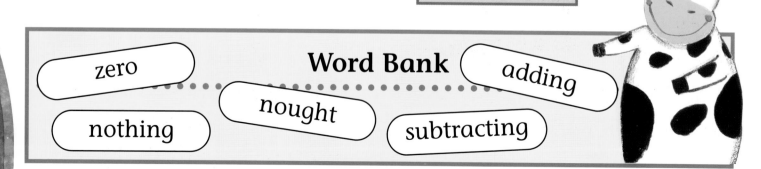

Did you know?

The signs **+**, **−**, and **=** have been used for hundreds of years.

+ was written on sacks of grain that were too heavy.

− was written on sacks of grain that were too light.

The first mathematician to use **=** was Robert Recorde.

The numbers we use to write sums came from India a long time ago.

1   2   3   4   5

6   7   8   9   10

Word Bank

Do you remember these words?
Can you find them in the book?

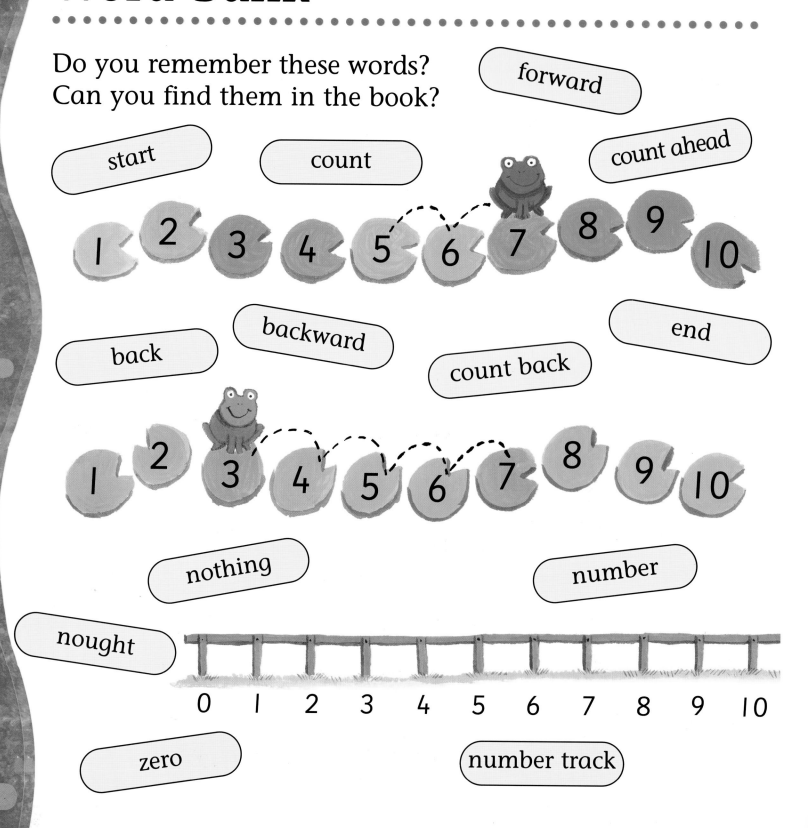

forward

start

count

count ahead

back

backward

count back

end

nothing

number

nought

zero

number track

Word Bank

same

pairs

larger

how many?

compare

less

more

score

Word Bank

subtraction

minus

subtracting

−2

3

5

leaves

take away

remove

subtract

leave

fewer

Word Bank

sum

makes

altogether

sign

totaling

plus

equals

add

total

adding

enter

+3

7

4

Adding and Subtracting Quiz

What is the score?

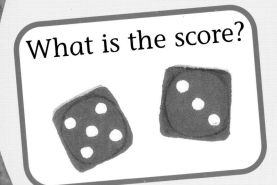

If 4 fly away, how many will be left?

How many more does Luke have?

Luke   Carla

What is the total?

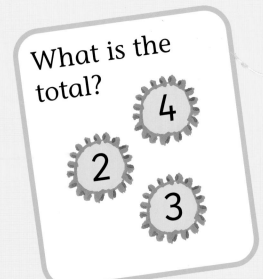

What is left if you subtract 0 from 6?

There should be 10 peas in the pod. How many are missing?